A Celebration of Old-Fashioned Gardens

GRANDMA'S
G · A · R · D · E · N

laura martin

LONGSTREET PRESS, INC.
Atlanta, Georgia

To the loving memory of
Grandpa and Grandma Skaggs

Published by
LONGSTREET PRESS, INC.
a subsidiary of Cox Newspapers,
a subsidiary of Cox Enterprises, Inc.
2140 Newmarket Parkway
Suite 118
Marietta, Georgia 30067

2nd printing, 1994

Library of Congress Catalog Number 90-061854

ISBN 0-929264-41-X

This book was printed by Eerdmans Printing Company, Grand Rapids, Michigan. The text type was set in Bembo by Typo-Repro Service, Inc., Atlanta, Georgia. Design by Paulette Livers Lambert.

Photo credits
Atlanta Historical Society: page 97. Cherokee Library, Atlanta Historical Society: pages 31, 32, 37, 38, 53, 54, 55, 79, 123. Georgia Department of Archives and History, Atlanta, Georgia: pages 3, 4, 9, 46, 70, 104, 107, 110, 113, 114. Great Smoky Mountain National Park Archives, Gatlinburg, Tennessee: pages 10, 11, 67, 105, 109, 135. Forest Service Collection, National Agricultural Library, Plimouth Plantation, Plymouth, Massachusetts: pages 86, 131.

Table of Contents

Introduction

Ever since the time of Adam, grandmothers appear to have been making gardens and their grandchildren making invidious comparisons with the gardens they see. It's a pretty poor grandchild who can't boast an expert gardener for a grandmother.

That legendary grandmother was always in her garden—she worked in it, and she sat in it, and she enjoyed it. . . . Perhaps it was because we always found her there that we have such pleasant memories of grandmother's garden.

—Richardson Wright,
A Small House and Large Garden (1924)

Almost anyone who loves gardening or the idea of gardening can remember some garden, some patch of flowers or row of vegetables, that served as an early inspiration. Like many memories, these gardens of our minds have taken on almost mystical properties over time. Were Grandma's hollyhocks really saucer-sized? Were Grandpa's corn and beans really the best we've ever eaten? Even allowing for memory's revision and the passage of decades, the answers to these questions may well be a hearty yes!

Gardens were very important to our ancestors, for both the beauty and the produce they supplied. The vegetable garden was more often than not necessary to ensure that the family had enough to eat. Herbs from the kitchen garden were used as medicines and flavorings and to scent Grandma's drawers.

But beyond necessity, the garden was a source of pride and pleasure. In summer Grandma lined the front porch with beautiful exotic plants—for her own enjoyment, of course, but also for their prominent position, which guaranteed that friends and neighbors would see visible evidence of her green thumb.

The front garden was always meticulous. Lilies and hollyhocks glowed against the white picket fence. Sweet William lined the walk. The lilac bush at the corner of the house gave off its unforgettable fragrance. The ever-present rose climbed high over the fence, spilling into the neighbor's yard—the only hint that everything was not exactly in its proper place.

The back garden was relaxed and happy-go-lucky in comparison. Here Grandma grew flowers and herbs for cooking and doctoring. Here she picked blossoms for potpourri and tussie-mussies. Here she chose blossoms to hang upside down in the attic to dry.

Without access to horticultural information that is standard today, Grandma had to depend on superstition and folk wisdom to determine when and how to plant. The moon and zodiac signs played a big part in the decision about when to plant, and folk wisdom passed down from earlier generations dictated plant care. Chemical fertilizers and pesticides were unknown, so Grandma depended on what she had on hand. Kitchen scraps were used as fertilizers. Household soaps and powders took care of pests and insects.

Because the garden was such an integral part of family life, it was only natural that community celebrations grew up around significant garden events. When too much garden work for a single family piled up, a corn shuckin', berry stemmin', or apple peelin' was held, and many hands finished the task in short order. Then came the party or dance. Harvest was the year's main celebration time. Folks gathered to share their bounty and rejoice.

With urbanization, we have lost many of the joys of the rural community. But the magic of an old-fashioned garden has never left our collective memory. *Grandma's Garden* is a book of nostalgia, an explanation of how and why our grandmothers gardened. Cultivating those plants that Grandma grew fills us with a sweet sense of continuity, connection to our past.

Grandma's Garden explores the ways our forebears designed and maintained their patches, plots, and portions of land. We have come full circle. Because of today's environmental concerns, we have to take a long, hard look at current gardening practices. No longer are harmful chemicals acceptable in the garden. No longer can we spray poison into the air to eliminate pests. We must find alternatives, and in looking forward we look back—to Grandma's garden.

Many of her old-fashioned methods are proving their effectiveness in today's newfangled gardens. Natural fertilizers, companion planting, and organic pest control are all old solutions to ageless problems. In adopting these old methods, we are returning to a simpler way of gardening, one more closely tied to the soil and one that makes us an integral part of life's web.

WHY WE GARDEN

Grandma stood up slowly, her back bent from hours of leaning over the flower bed. Carefully she straightened, one hand on her knee, the other on her hip, and grimaced as her bones creaked and complained about assuming a new position.

The sun beat down unmercifully. She removed her hat and wiped her wet brow with a lace handkerchief stuck in the bosom of her blouse. Her hands, gnarled and weathered, were evidence of years of gardening in the sun. The wrinkles lining her face spoke of age and wisdom.

Slowly, she hobbled to a nearby bench and sighed heavily as she dropped her body onto it. She put her hat back on her head and looked around. The grimace became a smile. Her eyes twinkled with joy as she surveyed her garden.

She turned to me. "It's a good garden, Laura. The good Lord and I have done a lot of work here."

In all the years I watched Grandma work in her garden, she seemed never to tire. Hour after hour she would weed and water, plant and nurture. At the end of a long day in the hot sun, she would sit and behold the fruits of her labors with obvious pride.

What is it about a garden that can make us forget the aching back, the soiled knees? What is it about digging in the dirt that erases the memory of scratches and bug bites and calloused fingers? Why do we garden? Why do we put up with the unpredictable moods of Mother Nature? Why do we silently accept the ravages of storms and drought and patiently plant again? Why do we sweat in the sun for vegetables that we could, with much less effort, buy at the local store?

Though our specific answers might be different, all of us who dig in the dirt share an unbreakable bond, a camaraderie unique to gardeners. Put two gardeners together and they will never run out of things to say. From dirt to rain, blossoms to fruit, the elements of gardening are rooted deep in the lives of gardeners, shaping their moods and coloring their emotions.

In 1915 Mrs. Francis King wrote in *The Well-Considered Garden,* "If my eye lights upon the carefully tended [garden] at once I experience the warmest feeling of friendliness for that householder, and wish to know and talk with them about their flowers. For at the bottom there is a bond which breaks down every other difference between us. We are 'Garden Souls.'"

Produce has little to do with why today's gardeners garden. Supermarkets, farmer's markets, and flower shops can supply anyone with fresh fruits, vegetables, and flowers. Although the vegetable garden in Grandma's day was more necessary than it is today, she went beyond what was essential to putting food on the table. Herbs and flowers graced the garden beside her kitchen door. Flowering trees and shrubs added delicate charm to her lawn.

To put monetary value on a garden is impossible. Henry David Thoreau said, "Many men go fishing all of their lives without knowing that it is not fish they are after." The same could be said of gardeners. We do not garden for the produce; we garden for the sheer joy of growing things.

Creating and caring for a garden is work, hard, physical labor, yet the most delicate, refined ladies have found pleasure in shoveling dirt and pulling weeds. More than a thousand years ago a Chinese poet wrote:

> *Magical power,*
> *marvelous action!*
> *Chopping wood,*
> *carrying water.*

The poet's point is that spiritual growth can come from performing everyday tasks. Chopping wood, carrying water—or pulling weeds and shoveling dirt—are lowly jobs that could be done by anyone. But those who leave themselves open to the broader possibilities inherent in such menial tasks will discover their restorative and uplifting powers. Anyone can *do* these things. It takes a special sensitivity to realize their highest rewards.

Love of gardening seems partially hereditary, partially environmental. Those lucky enough to be born into a family of hoers and planters rarely turn their backs on the gardening life. Recent converts try, with a good bit of zeal, to convert others. An inescapable, pleasurable necessity for some, gardening is important to others primarily as something—whether knowledge or produce—to share with family and friends.

Bill Bricker, a gardening friend from Augusta, Georgia, says, "I garden because I love to watch things grow. I love to experiment with new varieties. I love to dig in rich soil filled with living things. I love to grow big bragging-size plants and share them with my friends and neighbors."

Perhaps it is a form of bragging, giving away the most beautiful or largest items from your garden. Perhaps it is the sincere desire to give someone else the best you have produced. But sharing from your garden is always sharing yourself. You give of your time and effort, dreams and heartaches.

When we plant for future generations, we are certainly planting out of a love for Earth and a desire to leave it a better place. A Jewish folktale describes an old man of "seventy years and seven" who spent many of his days digging in the earth. A young boy came to him one day and asked what he was planting. The man told him it was a breadfruit tree. The boy asked, "And when will your tree bear fruit?" The old man answered, "In seventeen years and seven."

The young boy looked at him in surprise. "Surely you cannot expect to live long enough to see the tree bear fruit. Why would you plant this?" he asked. The old man pondered his question before he said, "When I came into this world, there were trees here for me. It is my duty to make sure that when I leave there will be trees here also."

So perhaps we seed the soil out of a sense of responsibility. Perhaps we work the land to satisfy a basic need to connect with the

earth. Perhaps to dig in the dirt is a bond with ancient ancestors whose very lives depended on their relationship with the earth. Perhaps we garden because we *need* that connection with the elements. Perhaps as stewards of our earth, we garden to establish a partnership with Mother Nature. Perhaps we continue to garden long after our weary bones beg for rest because this digging and planting keeps us young. Every seed that we plant is an act of faith: that the seeds will grow, that the sun will shine and the rains will come, that we will be able to reap a harvest and become part of the never-ending cycles of nature.

SPRING

Grandma and I sat on the front porch and looked out over the newly plowed garden. It was early spring. The wind still had a definite chill. Grandma pulled her sweater closer around her thin shoulders and waved her hand toward the garden.

"It's the land of opportunity," she said. "Just smell it! There's no other smell like it in the world."

I sniffed, tentatively at first, then more enthusiastically as the odor of fresh-tilled soil filled my nostrils.

"This is the real smell of spring," Grandma told me.

Spring is about hopes and dreams. In spring ravages of bugs and pests, of drought or a late frost are merely unpleasant memories from seasons past. In spring anything is possible.

Spring brings the family together out-of-doors. After a housebound winter, everyone is ready and anxious for escape, and the garden becomes a natural gathering place. There are chores for everyone. Small hands carry away sticks and branches that have fallen in winter storms, making way for bigger hands to turn the earth. Young and old hands work together to pull stubborn stumps from the field. Soft, smooth hands work with hardened ones to plant tiny, fragile shoots of vegetables and flowers. All hands join together to pray for gentle rains and plenty of sunshine so that the plants will grow and produce.

Although each season has its own magic, once you've experienced spring in a garden, no other experience will quite compare.

Shirley Vogler experienced her first spring in the north Georgia mountains after having lived in Florida for thirty-one years. She and her husband grew homesick for the Virginia mountains of their childhoods but were unwilling to move quite that far north. So they did the next-best thing and moved to Talking Rock, Georgia.

"Everyone told us that we'd only have two bad months [January and February], but we hit the coldest winter they'd ever had and it was long!" Shirley says. "Anyway, our first real spring in many years was a glory to behold. Daffodils and tulips popped up everywhere. Then there were the peonies, snowball bushes, roses, yellow bells, spirea, rose of Sharon, apple trees, and much more. We really knew we'd bought ourselves a *home*."

Although home is where you hang your hat to many folks, to others home is where you set your trowel. If home is the place to gather the family, to work and play together, to share in chores and reap the benefits of hard work, then to many of us the garden *is* more of a home than the house is.

Shirley goes on to say, "I thank God my father loved gardening and passed that on to me. Every year he'd try something new, and although I'm not a very good gardener, I still enjoy digging in the dirt."

That's what gardening is all about: digging in the dirt. Someone suggested that gardeners are only adults who still love to play in the

dirt. To feel soft, loose dirt run through your fingers or to hold sun-warmed soil in the palm of your hand is a sensation hard to match for pleasure or potential.

Of course, not everyone is thrilled about spending spring afternoons doing garden chores. Marjorie Luce told me about planting corn in Oregon when she was a child. She said, "My sister and I were sent to plant hills of corn. Mother told us how and how many to plant. . . . We became tired and returned much sooner than Mother had thought possible. She knew why when, instead of five or six corn plants appearing, each hill was a little corn forest. It was too late for a good spanking, but we never did that again!"

Never plant on the new moon or on a day the moon changes.

WHEN TO PLANT

Gardeners have always questioned when to plant. Many old wives' tales and superstitions about spring planting exist. One of the more interesting is the belief that gardeners who stood naked while planting would raise better plants. In *Old Wives' Tales for Gardeners* Maureen and Bridget Boland write, "The best husbandmen would have the seedsman of turnips or grapes to be naked when he sows them, and in sowing to protest that this which he doth is for himself and his neighbours." The theory behind this belief held that the gods would look more favorably upon the naked and the innocent and give special attention to their gardens.

PLANTING BY THE MOON AND SIGNS

Bill Bricker is an extraordinary gardener. All of his plants are grown in raised beds and fed with organic fertilizers. But the sheer size and beauty of his plants make you wonder if he hasn't concocted some magic to create the produce he does every year. When asked about his success, Bill smiles slyly and admits to planting by the moon and by zodiac signs.

"I can't really believe all that's said about planting by the signs," he confides, "but there is too much evidence to disbelieve. I have a good friend, Walter Wison, who is a professional gardener, and he always plants by the signs for good reason. He gets more fruit, better roots, better everything.

"My dad and granddad and a host of others followed the signs when they planted. They also followed the signs when they set fence posts or killed trees or a lot of other farm chores. Have you ever dug a hole and planted a post and still didn't have enough dirt to fill the hole back up? It's all because of the pull of gravity. There's just too much evidence to disbelieve."

A lot of gardening folks agree with Bill. We might not understand it all, but if it works, why not use it?

Planting by the signs:

- **Beets in the third quarter under Cancer, Scorpio, Pisces, Libra, or Capricorn**
- **Broccoli in the first quarter under Cancer, Scorpio, or Pisces**
- **Cabbage in the first quarter under Cancer, Scorpio, Pisces, Taurus, or Libra**
- **Cantaloupe in the first and second quarter under Cancer, Scorpio, Pisces, or Libra**
- **Carrots in the third quarter under Cancer, Scorpio, Pisces, or Libra**
- **Corn in the first quarter under Cancer, Scorpio, or Pisces**
- **Cucumbers in the first quarter under Gemini**
- **Lettuce in the first quarter under Cancer, Scorpio, Pisces, or Libra**
- **Onions in the second quarter under Scorpio or Sagittarius**
- **Sweet peas in the second quarter under Virgo (English peas planted then will produce great blossoms and little fruit)**
- **English peas in the second quarter under Cancer, Scorpio, Pisces, or Libra**
- **Squash in the second quarter under Cancer, Scorpio, Pisces, or Libra**
- **Tomatoes in the second quarter under Cancer, Scorpio, or Pisces**
- **Crops planted during Taurus and Cancer will withstand drought**

Plant in the spring:
- **when hepatica blooms in the woods**
- **when pin cherry leaves are as big as a squirrel's ear**
- **when the shadbush is in bloom**
- **when apple blossoms drop**
- **when hickory leaves are as big as a crow's feet**
- **when cherry trees are in bloom**

Plant:
- **beans, watermelons, gourds, and fruit on Good Friday**
- **potatoes on Memorial Day**
- **corn three to seven days before the average last frost or when apple leaves are as big as a mouse's ear**

Bill Kaheley, an old-fashioned gardener extraordinaire, says it's sort of like keeping lions out of the garden. You have to clap your hands real loud. If you don't see any lions, you'd better keep clapping because it's obviously working.

Planting by the signs is not strictly for the older gardener. As Clyde Lester, a county extension agent, points out, "Age really has nothing to do with it because a lot of young gardeners use the methods. Plenty of generations before us did and we got fat, so I can't quarrel with it."

Sometimes gardeners can become a little confused about *which* signs to follow. An eighty-five-year-old woman who always has a good garden follows the "signs" on her Rexall drugstore calendar. "See the fish?" she says. "Whenever it says 'best,' that's when I plant." That the signs she used referred to the best fishing days seemed to matter very little to her or to her garden. In fact, many of the best fishing days are also the best planting days, according to the signs of the zodiac. In *Planetary Planting* Louise Riotte says, "All nature dances to the rhythm of the music of the spheres."

The pull of the moon, which causes the tides, is present in all bodies of water, no matter how small. To newly planted seeds, moisture is everything, and the miniscule tides within the earth give new seeds the extra advantage that can make the difference in their productivity. The full moon causes moisture in the soil to rise closer to the earth's surface. Newly planted crops, thirsty for any bit of water, can profit from this brief cyclical surge.

Gardeners also plant by the phases of the zodiac. The twelve signs have each eventually become associated with specific gardening characteristics. Some are thought to be beneficial to planting, others to harvest, still others to killing weeds and other pests.

For gardeners interested in planting by the moon or zodiac signs, almost all almanacs contain planting calendars, giving suggestions as to when to plant which crops. Among the best sources are *Llewellyn's Astrological Calendar* (Llewellyn Publications, St. Paul, MN 55164-0383) and *Planting by the Moon* (Astro Computing Services, San Diego, CA 92116).

NATURAL FERTILIZERS

My mother had a compost pile long before it was in vogue. One of my least favorite childhood chores was taking kitchen scraps down to the woods to add to the pile. Holding my nose, I would take cantaloupe rinds, eggshells, coffee grounds—enough to fill a bowl—down the path. In spite of my disgust at having to transport smelly garbage, I watched with wonder as the scraps from our kitchen turned into rich, black dirt.

It didn't happen overnight, of course, and not everything turned to dirt with the same speed. Banana peels rotted almost instantly, but eggshells and Mom's biscuits seemed to stay around for years. Once the creepy, crawly critters did their work and nature had transformed kitchen scraps into black gold, the compost worked magic on our garden. The overworked red clay soil hungrily consumed the compost. Wherever we put it, vegetables were plumper, flowers more beautiful.

Today the family compost pile has taken on a new importance. It not only provides safe nutrients for the soil, reducing the need for chemical fertilizers, but also supplies an environmentally sound receptacle for much household and garden trash. Grass clippings and other lawn and garden debris make up a substantial portion of household refuse. Because landfills are quickly reaching their capacity, it is more and more crucial for us to reuse and recycle whatever we can to reduce the amount of garbage that we produce.

When I visited the Kaheleys' garden west of Atlanta, they greeted me like a long-lost cousin. I stood with Bill Kaheley, looked over his garden, and listened intently to his stories. Black soil showed between neat rows of lettuce and broccoli. Tiny corn stalks were just beginning to peep above ground.

"When we first moved here, this land was terribly eroded. There were gullies so wide we couldn't even get a tractor across," Bill said. Then he laughed and shook his head. "The good Lord gives some folks good soil, but those with enough patience, he gives us poor soil, and we just have to work with it and make the best of it. I guess the Lord thought that I was just full of patience."

That patience has paid off. After years of work and truckloads of topsoil, compost, and organic matter, he has a showplace garden.

Feeding the soil is not exactly a new idea although the use of commercial fertilizers is a relatively recent method. Not everyone likes or trusts the new fertilizers. In *Cabbagetown Families, Cabbagetown Food* Azilee Edwards writes, "The onliest difference in food now and when I was a child, they fertilize the ground so much till stuff grows so fast it takes the taste out of it. Now when I was little they let the nature of the ground take the course, you see. They'd wait till the right time of year to plant the gardens and everything had a better flavor. . . .

"Now onions like those back years ago, those would be delicious. But I bet you could go out and pull one now and it'd be right slimy like, you know, watery on account of the fertilizer."

The natural fertilizers available to gardeners in earlier days have their scientific bases. Barnyard manure and kitchen scraps work not by magic, but by chemistry. Corn stalks serve as ventilators to get more air into the compost. Banana peels, chopped fine, add phosphorus to the compost pile. The chopped peelings can also be buried around tomatoes, eggplant, peppers, and roses. Because they break down so quickly, they provide quick calcium, magnesium, sulphur, phosphates, sodium, and silica to the places the plants are growing.

Coffee grounds, placed around melons and carrots, add nutrients,

Sunday is the sun's day. It is hot and barren. Do not plant on this day.

attract earthworms, and repel pests. Eggshells, over a period of a few years, add lime, nitrogen, and phosphorus to the soil. Wood ash, full of potash, is a good fertilizer for cabbage, potatoes, onions, strawberries, fruit trees, corn, and beans in the vegetable garden and hydrangeas, carnations, roses, and peonies in the flower garden. (Wood ash, however, should not be placed around germinating seeds.)

A nineteenth-century gardener says of soot tea, another popular fertilizer, "I place about a peck of soot in a half barrel in some convenient place near the garden, fill this with water and use it once a week around the roots of the roses, thoroughly wetting the ground with it."

Some of the fertilizers used in Grandma's time are impractical for today's gardener. For example, an 1870 magazine article suggests using horses' hoofs to improve the soil: "Put one bushel of the clippings from horses' hoofs into a barrel and fill it up with water. Let it stand for a week, when it is fit for use. Apply it with a watering pot." Grandma even tossed her old boots and shoes onto the compost heap. Once they rotted, their leather was supposed to release all sorts of things good for the garden.

Surprisingly enough, salt was sometimes used as a fertilizer in Grandma's day. In 1840 Henry Ward Beecher said, "Salt may be used

"I've learned that success with house plants, my dear, means FEEDING THEM"!

with great advantage on all garden soils, but especially upon light and sandy ones. Thus treated, soils will resist summer droughts and stay moist when otherwise they would suffer. Salt has also a good effect in destroying vermin, and its adds valuable chemical ingredients to the soil." An 1864 *Farmer's Almanac* suggests mixing seven bushels of salt with seven bushels of soot to be plowed into one acre of ground.

Epsom salt was scratched into the soil then watered well to correct magnesium deficiency. A small amount of salt placed in planting holes for tomatoes, peppers, and eggplant was thought to be quite beneficial as well.

Another somewhat surprising plant nutrient is camphor, used for houseplants and cut flowers. The July 1924 issue of *Garden* magazine reported, "A small amount of camphor in the water also tends to stimulate the absorption of water by the stems, which is a desirable thing. The inexperienced will think that salt and hot water are the last things to use to revive faded flowers, but in fact nothing is better."

COLLECTING AND SAVING HEIRLOOM PLANTS

The most prized possession in my yard would be worth exactly twelve dollars to anyone else, that being the amount it would take to buy a good peony plant. The value of this particular peony, however, has nothing to do with money. My peony is priceless, for it came from a tiny division from my mother's plants, which in turn came from her mother's garden.

When I watch the matchless glory of our peony, I wonder at the continuity of the garden that transcends time and bridges the gap between generations. To have a bit of my grandmother's garden growing at my doorstep brings me inexplicable happiness.

A friend living in Louisiana has a patchwork quilt of a garden. To her, a plant's origin is more important than the plant itself, and certainly more important than the overall design of her garden. She boasts irises from her mother, a pawpaw tree from her grandfather, wild petunias from a friend now dead.

Generosity is a strong characteristic in almost all gardeners. Sharing plants with family and friends is a marvelous privilege. To pass plants on from one generation to another sends ancestral roots even deeper into both hearts and soil.

Many gardeners today mistakenly think that bigger is better. Catalogues boast of plants that are taller, fuller, more fragrant, beautiful, or delicious. Although the world of plant breeding is exciting and the wonders of science impressive, all the glossy pictures and three-dollar-words sometimes make us sigh wistfully and long for the simple plants that Grandma used to grow.

Our ancestors had some of the most visually stunning gardens to be seen anywhere, without the benefit of hybrids or "new improved strains." The large, simple flowers from Grandma's garden brought great pleasure to generations of folks and have not lost any of their charm today.

Whatever happened to Alma Gem melons or Howling Mob corn? In their time they were considered premier varieties. Howling Mob got its name because farmers who came into town to sell this variety were quickly surrounded by a howling mob wanting to buy.

FEED THE SOIL AND IT WILL FEED YOU

But, in spite of their one-time popularity, many of these varieties are now preserved only in agricultural journal articles.

Modern gardeners assume that Grandma had only a few varieties from which to choose and that her choices are all still available today, along with the multitude of new hybrids and strains. The truth is that gardeners at the turn of the century enjoyed tremendous variety, but, unfortunately, many of these strains are now lost. For example, in 1900 there were approximately two hundred varieties of beans available to farmers. Less than 20 percent have survived. Some have been abandoned in favor of new versions with improved taste or greater resistance to disease. Others have been lost because they were difficult to pick or gather and not suited to mechanized harvesting. Other strains declined because they adapted to very narrow environmental ranges and were thus unsuitable for mass marketing.

The modern gardener might well ask what difference these losses make. Aren't the newer varieties bigger and better adapted to our needs?

The answers are mixed.

Certainly the newer strains produce larger fruits and vegetables. But is bigger necessarily better? The older varieties had characteristics that made them quite valuable to the home gardener. For example, some older strains exhibit greater tolerance to drought and cold temperatures or show a better ability to grow in poor soils and resist disease.

There is no way to predict every horticultural need, and many of these older fruit and vegetable varieties might contain characteristics that will be essential to our future health and welfare. This potential is in itself argument enough for fighting to preserve all strains of these heirloom plants. When a particular variety becomes extinct, it is gone forever, and the unique combination of genes that created that particular plant can never be recaptured. It is important that plant diversity be maintained, for our present needs and for other future needs we can't anticipate with complete accuracy.

In addition to the philosophical and ethical reasons for maintaining crop and plant diversity, there are personal reasons as well. Some folks simply like the way that old-fashioned fruits and vegetables look and taste. Although older varieties can be tougher or stringier, many prefer their tastes and work hard to preserve them. Other gardeners grow older vegetable and fruit varieties out of curiosity. The imaginative possibilities in Fat Horses beans or Moon and Stars watermelon, for example, make growing them almost irresistible.

Other folks grow heirloom vegetables for more sentimental reasons. Kent Whealy, director of the Seed Saver's Exchange, began his love affair with heirloom plants when his grandfather gave him a wedding present of seeds for a pink potato-leaved tomato, a prolific pole bean, and a deep purple morning glory with a red star center. These seeds were from plants that had been brought from Bavaria by his ancestors four generations earlier. When his grandfather died the winter after giving him the seeds, Kent realized that he had been entrusted with a unique and precious family heirloom.

There are great advantages to saving seeds of both modern and heirloom varieties. They are free, and if gardeners are selective about which seeds they save, these varieties will eventually adapt to particular tastes, soils, and climates.

Gardeners must keep each line of heirloom varieties separate. They cannot be allowed to crossbreed. This separation can be of either time or space: the strains can be planted on a schedule that means they will not bloom during the same period, or they can be placed far enough apart that they cannot exchange pollen.

Finding heirloom plants can be challenging and fun. It just might become a Sunday afternoon passion. Start close to home and search out abandoned homesites. Don't neglect "weedy"-looking plants. A little selective pruning can do wonders for an old-fashioned plant.

The Seed Saver's Exchange is an important source of seeds for heirloom fruits and vegetables. Members of this nonprofit organization save and swap seeds from older vegetable varieties. The Exchange lives up to its name, for members do just that: trade seeds with the organization's help. Although seeds are available for sale, they are expensive by design, the aim of the organization being to encourage gardeners to find, grow, and share old varieties without any money changing hands. The Exchange has no intention of functioning as a commercial seed company. Anyone with seeds to share can become a member, and members may order seeds from each other for the price of postage. The Garden Seed Inventory put out by the Exchange lists 5,785 non-hybrid vegetables offered in the United States and Canada.

For information about the organization, send a self-addressed, stamped envelope to Seed Saver's Exchange, 203 Rural Avenue, Decorah, Iowa 52101.

"*Wonderful!*"—
It's the

Sowrite Seed-Sower

Sows Seeds at a Touch!

Each Plant Comes Up Separately
NO WASTE OF SEED, TIME OR PLANTS

The Amateur Gardener, with this instrument, is now able to sow the finest seeds with a precision and assurance of success hitherto possible only to the skilled professional.

PEST CONTROL

Grandma threw the rock with a precision that could have come only from years of practice. Although she missed the big black crow by several inches, he cawed and cackled, then rose up from the strawberry bed in a flurry of indignation.

I turned to Grandma, impressed. "Where did you learn to throw like that?"

She chuckled. "Uncle Alvie and I used to sit on the front porch by the hour keeping the birds out of the fruit. It got to be sort of a game for us. He always thought that he was a better shot, just because he was a boy. But I guess I proved him wrong." She laughed again. "We used to keep score. You got five points for actually hitting the old crows and two points if you made them fly off." She stopped and rubbed her shoulder. "I guess I'm a little out of practice now, but I bet I could still beat Uncle Alvie!

"We weren't just kidding around, either. Your great-grandfather loved his strawberry patch, and we were held accountable if the birds got into the berries. I guess it was 'cause we were the youngest that we got the job of being a scarecrow. We got pretty good at it, too.

"My ma would take those strawberries and on Sunday afternoon we would all pitch in and make homemade ice cream. Talk about good! I'm telling you there was nothing like it in the world. She used to drop whole berries into the mixer, and they'd get all icy. But they were the sweetest berries I've ever tasted."

Because the garden feels like home to so many of us, we sometimes surprise even ourselves with the ferocity with which we protect it. Only if you have lost prized tomatoes to midnight marauders or an entire strawberry patch to a passing flock of birds can you know the heartache and helplessness of a gardener robbed. After all, you can always call the police if your house if burglarized, but who will come to your rescue if your garden is ransacked?

Not all critters that rob gardens are four-legged. Shirley Vogler confesses to garden-robbing when she was a youngster. "My family moved to the suburbs when I was sixteen. Soon I was in a 'gang,' which included all of the kids from our street and some from the next street. I wasn't there long when five or six of the kids decided it would be fun to slip into Mr. Robinson's strawberry patch for some strawberries.

"It was a pretty moonlit night, and I was ready to be part of the gang. We slipped into the strawberry patch and were feeling around for the berries when Mr. Robinson opened his front door, stepped onto the porch, and looked around! The garden ran parallel to the house, so they all took off for the back of the garden, with me running last. They hadn't told me that there was a fence that hit you at hip-height. Well, you can guess what happened. I hit that fence at full speed and hung over! Half of me on one side and half on the other. There I was rocking back and forth like a rag doll.

"They all came back to help me, but I was laughing so hard that I couldn't move! They finally got hold of my feet and toppled me over to the other side. We all had a good laugh out of it, but I don't think any of us ever went back into that strawberry patch again. I always believed that Mr. Robinson knew we were there all the time. My father would have been on me like a duck on a June bug if he'd known I was there."

Keeping bugs and critters out of the garden has always been a big problem for the gardener. Most of us are pretty philosophical about it. Nell Glass always plants enough for the bugs too, calling it "paying dues to Mother Nature." The decision to share your garden with critters of the field and forest is not always left up to you. Rabbits, deer, squirrels, birds, moles, chipmunks, and anything else that flies, hops, or crawls will want a piece of your garden.

Almost all gardeners will admit that the easiest method of controlling pests and disease is keeping healthy plants. This means persistent care. Once weeds get out of hand or the plants dry out, the damage is done. A neat garden will certainly be freer of pests than a neglected one. Weeds rob plants of space and nutrients, and the closeness of the plants causes mildew and a ripe environment for the spread of disease.

Grandma's methods for handling unwanted garden guests varied from ingenious to sneaky to downright impossible. Some folks, for example, thought sprinkling lion dung around roses would keep deer from nibbling on the young shoots. The only catch here was finding a steady source of lion dung!

One keep-clean is worth a dozen make-cleans. — *Ozark proverb*

WILSON'S O. K. PLANT SPRAY

Azilee Edwards says, "Everybody I know's got a little patch of some kind, growing some kind of vegetables. You name it and we got it. I used to use Bruton snuff on bugs. I'd take and sprinkle it on the buds of any kind of plant that's buggy. . . . Mostly I just let the bugs have the right of way."

Many of Grandma's pest control methods have wonderful applications for us today. Because chemical controls are harmful to the environment, gardeners are always searching for effective, harmless methods for dealing with pests.

GRANDMA'S REMEDIES FOR LARGER PESTS

General
• Sprinkle cayenne pepper on corn silks and foliage of beans, tomato plants, and other crops to keep away all kinds of creatures.

Ants
• Pour boiling water down the entrance to the anthill.
• Sprinkle sulfur on the affected plants.
• Sprinkle a few leaves of green wormwood around black ant hills.

Birds
• Hang bits of onion in fruit trees to keep birds away.
• Spray with a weak salt solution to keep birds away from cherries.

Caterpillars
• Boil together rue, wormwood, and cheap tobacco. The liquid will be strong. Sprinkle it on leaves and young branches of trees every morning and evening during the time fruit is ripening.

Cutworms
• Press broken eggshells into the soil around plants.
• Place a small band of cardboard (a toilet paper roll, paper towel roll, or milk carton) one inch into the ground around the young plant, leaving two inches above ground.
• Place a nail or toothpick alongside a plant's stem.
• Sprinkle around plants with equal parts of salt, ashes, and plaster of Paris.

Deer
• Put half a bar of old-fashioned plain soap into a "knee-hi" stocking and suspend it from a three-foot stake. Place one of these every six feet or so.
• Human hair cuttings, wrapped in a piece of stocking and hung from a post, will deter deer.
• To keep deer out of the corn, apply several drops of mineral oil to corn silks as soon as they begin to dry and turn brown. (Do not do this before pollination or the plants will not develop correctly.) Apply the oil three times a day at five-day intervals.
• Dip a thick cloth in creosote and put it at the end of a stake. Place these stakes throughout the garden.

Dogs
• If a dog digs in the garden, place mothball crystals in the holes it digs.

Flies
• Mix black pepper with cream and sugar. Place around plants.
• Repel flies with rue, pennyroyal, sage, tansy, or spearmint.

Fruit worms
• Store fruit with sassafras, a large handful per bushel of fruit.

Gophers
• Plant scilla bulbs in both the flower and vegetable gardens.
• Place one of the following in their holes: (1) rags soaked in olive oil; (2) dog droppings; or (3) a child's pinwheel (they don't like the vibrations).

Lice
• To cut down on lice on livestock, allow animals to stand out in the first rain of May.

Moles
• Place one of the following in their holes: (1) rags soaked in olive oil; (2) dog droppings; or (3) a child's pinwheel (they don't like the vibrations).
• Bury a quart-sized pop bottle half full of water at an angle. The wind will cause a whistling sound that will scare them away.
• Plant castor beans in their holes.
• Place sprigs from elder trees in mole runs.
• Put a few castor oil beans in each hole and cover.
• Keep an interested and persistent cat.

Raccoons
• To keep raccoons out of the corn, plant pumpkin seeds about four feet apart in the corn field. As the corn matures, the big pumpkin leaves grow around the base of the stalks. Raccoons need to look around as they eat, and the pumpkin leaves prevent this.

Rabbits
• Plant onions among other plants.
• Short lengths of cut garden hose placed among plants to resemble snakes will scare rabbits away.
• Bury a quart-sized pop bottle half full of water at an angle. The wind will cause a whistling sound that will scare them away.
• Sprinkle talcum powder or flour on the foliage of beans and tomato seedlings.
• Sprinkle blood meal around plants.

Squirrels
• A few mothballs will keep squirrels out of your birdfeeder.

If one can put up with the particularly unpleasant odor of whale oil soap, this is excellent for keeping bugs out of the garden. — *William N. White (1868)*

Smaller pests, such as insects, present a different challenge to the gardener. Margaret Miller uses the "pick-and-smash method, or the knock-and-splash system." This means she spends a great deal of time actually picking bugs off her plants by hand, then releasing her frustrations by smashing them. If this isn't your favorite form of bug execution, carry a pail of kerosene along and simply drop the offenders into it.

Another form of bug control is a good hard spray of plain old water. Bill Bricker says, "Bugs are like kids. They don't like to be bathed." Water knocks many of the bugs off the plants, and, sprayed forcibly, will dislodge aphids. Aphids are also attracted to the color yellow, so a bright yellow dishpan full of water in the garden can also help attract and drown these pests. Sprinkling water over plants will help with red spiders, too, because they like very dry conditions.

Although water itself is effective, adding things to it is even more so — a bit of tobacco or a little kerosene, for example. Grandma never threw out her wash or dish water. Instead, she used it to bathe her plants. This "grey" water served to soften the soil and repel bugs. (If you use dish water today, make sure that it doesn't contain harmful phosphates.)

Several kinds of soaps are considered particularly effective in repelling insect pests, including many commercially available "insecticidal soaps." Old-fashioned gardeners used strong lye soap to wash their plants, being careful not to do this during the hottest part of the day when the soap would literally burn the plants.

Not all critters in the garden are harmful — some actually aid the gardener. Bill Kaheley loves to tell the story of his ducks. "For years we tried to keep the Mucovy ducks down by the pond. We tried everything, but they insisted on coming up to the garden. One year we had a terrible infestation of Japanese beetles, and I noticed that the ducks just gobbled them up like candy."

Many other kinds of birds eat flying insects. Purple martins, in particular, are useful for this purpose. Ladybugs are well known for their voracious appetites. They can eat up to a hundred aphids a day. Toads are also good to have around. A hungry toad will eat about ten thousand insects in three months. To encourage toads in your garden, place a clay flower pot, upside down with a large hole in its side, near a pan of water.

EASY, HARMLESS REMEDIES FOR SPECIFIC PLANTS

Asparagus
• Put refuse pork or beef brine on plants. This enhances growth and destroys weeds.

Broccoli
• Tie on a net bonnet. Cut a circle from the netting and thread string through the outer edges. Place the bonnet over the plant; pull the string and tie. This protects the plant from flying, egg-laying insects.

Cabbage
• For white flies: Mix one cup of sour milk, one quart of water, and three tablespoons of flour. Spray the mixture on the cabbage plants.
• Tie on a net bonnet. Cut a circle from the netting and thread string through the outer edges. Place the bonnet over the plant; pull the string and tie. This protects the plant from flying, egg-laying insects.
• Spray with sage and thyme tea to prevent worms.

Cantaloupe
• Set each melon on a piece of cardboard and dust with wood ashes.

Cauliflower
• A small handful of soot at the root will prevent grubs.
• Spray with sea water, lime water, or soap suds. This also helps control grubs.

Chrysanthemums
• Sprinkle a bit of tobacco dust on plants.

Cucumbers
• Sprinkle the vine with tobacco and red pepper.
• Spray with a tea made from tobacco, elder leaves, walnut leaves, or hops.
• Plant before sunrise on May 1.

Eggplant
• Place ground red peppers at the base of the plant and also rub them on the leaves.

House plants
• Blow smoke through the foliage of plants with aphids. (Do not use this remedy in the garden. Smoking itself should not be done in the vegetable garden as tobacco smoke causes disease in tomato plants.)

Peas
• Spray garlic tea on black pea aphids.

Peach trees
• Place sawdust or wood chips around the base of the tree to repel grubs.

Roses
• To treat black spots, grind up several tomato leaves in the blender with a little water. To one pint of tomato leaves, add five pints of water and one ounce of cornstarch. Keep the mixture refrigerated. Spray roses once a week.

Squash
• Grind up plug tobacco and boil it with hot peppers. Place around plants.
• Soak seeds in kerosene overnight to prevent squash borer.

Tomatoes
• Place ashes on the plants to keep fleas off.
• Dust plants attacked by caterpillars with dry cayenne pepper.

Watermelon
• Plant before sunrise on May 1.

Companion planting is another environmentally sound approach to pest control. Almost all old-fashioned gardeners will tell you that you can keep away certain pests by planting herbs and flowers in the garden. Although this has been a common practice for many years, little scientific data has been collected to support the idea of companion planting. This lack of proof means little to the enthusiastic gardener who believes in companion planting. Try these combinations to repel insects:

> garlic near roses for aphids
> basil near beans for beetles
> parsley near asparagus for beetles
> nasturtiums for whiteflies and aphids
> marigolds for nematodes
> tobacco for flea beetles
> catnip and tansy for squash bugs
> tansy for Colorado potato beetle
> mints for ants
> southernwood for cabbage butterflies
> rosemary for slugs and snails
> radishes for maggots near sprouting corn and cabbage
> parsley for rose beetles
> horseradish for potato beetles.

TYPICAL SPRING PLANTS FROM GRANDMA'S GARDEN

Common name: BLEEDING HEART
Botanical name: *Dicentra spectabilis*
Introduced: *D. eximia* (plumy bleeding heart) and *D. spectabilis* introduced to the U.S. between 1850 and 1900.
Description: Bleeding heart has a graceful arch of bright pink-and-white heart-shaped blossoms. The foliage is grey-green and fern-like. This species grows to a height of thirty inches.
How to grow: This is a wonderful plant to use in a shaded garden, for it performs best without direct sun. Open shade will give bleeding heart the best light conditions. It needs to be planted in rich, well-drained soil and should have ample moisture. It blooms in late spring.
How to use: Because it grows well in the shade, bleeding heart does well in a small woodland garden. It looks lovely if grown with ferns and small wildflowers such as dwarf-crested iris or woodland phlox.

England's Victorian gardeners loved bleeding heart. It complemented perfectly the romance and frills associated with that era. The plant was first introduced to England in 1846 by Robert Fortune, who found it growing on the Japanese island of Chusan.

Because of the unusual configuration of its blossom, bleeding heart has been given many different common names, including Our Lady in a boat, lyre flower, lady's locket, Chinaman's breeches, and lady in the bath.

Common name: CANDYTUFT
Botanical name: *Iberis umbellata*
Introduced: *I. amara* and *I. odorata* brought to the U.S. in the 1600s
Description: Candytuft is a low-growing annual that blooms in late spring and usually again in fall. The plant produces stems covered with bright green foliage and tiers of white or pink flower clusters. Each blossom measures only one-eighth to one-half inch across, and the entire plant rarely exceeds sixteen inches in height.
How to grow: Candytuft prefers full sun and plenty of moisture, although the soil should be well drained. Plants should be spaced twelve to fifteen inches apart. Candytuft can be propagated by dividing established plants, or seeds can be sown in spring after the last frost.
How to use: Because it is low-growing, candytuft makes an ideal edging plant or a filler in a perennial or mixed border. *Iberis sempervirens* is a perennial candytuft that grows well in full sun. The woody stems should be cut back after flowering to prevent dying out in the middle of the plant.

The name candytuft has nothing to do with candy. Instead, it refers to the original home of this plant—Candia, an old name for Crete. The genus name also refers to a place—Iberia—for many species of the genus are native to Iberia, or Spain.

There are many variations on the name candytuft, including candyedge and candyturf. Yet another old English name is Billy-come-home-soon.

Annual candytuft has been grown in gardens since 1596, but its perennial cousin did not appear in English gardens until the middle of the eighteenth century, when it was sent to Chelsea Gardens in London from Persia.

Candytuft is adaptable to a wide range of growing conditions, a characteristic that earned its place in the Oriental language of flowers as a symbol of indifference. Candytuft was also sometimes known as candy mustard, for some of the country folks used the seeds as a substitute in making mustard. It gained such a reputation for this that estate gardeners soon grew to look upon the plant with disdain and refused to include it within their own formal gardens. Although its medicinal uses are limited, candytuft was at one time made into a solution thought to be particularly soothing to those suffering from rheumatism.

A favorite old-fashioned variety is Empress.

Common name: CANTERBURY BELLS
Botanical name: *Campanula medium*
Introduced: Brought to U.S. in 1600s
Description: Sometimes called cup-and-saucer plant, the blossom of Canterbury bells is composed of petals, rolled on the edges, that form a bell-

shape with many conspicuous sepals. The colors are soft blues and pinks. It stands two to two-and-a-half feet tall and spreads twelve to eighteen inches across.

How to grow: This biennial takes a fair amount of effort and energy, but most gardeners agree that it is worth the time involved. It blooms during June, which is often considered a dead time in the garden. Canterbury bells should be started from seed in July or August. Sow seeds one-eighth inch deep and thin plants to twelve inches apart. In September transplant these to planting beds and mulch heavily to protect against winter cold. The tiny plants should then be moved to their permanent location in spring. This plant will bloom best if given at least half-day sun and will perform quite well in average garden soil.

How to use: The soft colors of Canterbury bells make it easy to use in planting beds with annuals or in a perennial border. Many colonial gardeners relied heavily on the soft pinks and blues of Canterbury bells to fill their gardens. Allowed to self-sow along with larkspur, poppies, and pinks, canterbury bells create a wonderful tapestry of color and fragrance.

During the mid-1700s this plant was routinely listed for sale in several northern newspapers. Canterbury bells were grown in this country much earlier, but the large number of common names used for the plant make definite identification difficult. Wild hyacinth, Venus's looking glass, lady's nightcap, Mercury violet, coventry bells, and bats-in-the-belfry are only a few of the names used to describe the plant. The name chimney bellflower was given to the plant because it was sometimes grown in pots and brought indoors to be placed in empty fireplaces during the summer months. By the nineteenth century canterbury bells were quite important to American gardeners.

Several species of *Campanulas* display a wonderful variety of colors and flower forms. One of the most legendary is *Campanula rapunculus,* the flower for which Rapunzul (from the Grimm fairy tale) was named. *Campanula rapunculus* was called English rampion and has been cultivated since the 1600s. Though considered a tasty vegetable, it might not be worth the risks involved in growing rampion in your garden. According to superstition, where rampion grows, children will be quarrelsome.

C. lactiflora, native to western Asia, was introduced to England in 1814 and was widely used in cottage gardens and gardens of fashionable country houses. *C. latifolia* was popular in Elizabethan and early Stuart gardens and could be found with both blue and white flowers.

Common name: COLUMBINE
Botanical name: *Aquilegia canadensis* — native to United States. Red and yellow blossoms twelve to twenty-four inches tall.
Aquilegia vulgaris — native to Europe. Pink, blue, mauve, white, or dark purple, single or double forms. Twenty-four to thirty-six inches tall.
Aquilegia caerulea — Colorado columbine, native to western United States. Blue and white blossoms. Twenty-four inches tall.
Introduced: Single and double varieties introduced to U.S. before the eighteenth century
Description: Columbines have attractive tri-lobed grey-green foliage. The

blossoms are bell-shaped and hang down daintily from the flowering stem. Each blossom has five reflexed spurs and five petals that point downward. Columbines generally bloom in June and July.

How to grow: Columbines prefer partial sun or light shade but will tolerate full sun if given sufficient moisture. The soil should be rich, full of humus, and well drained. Columbines are short-lived perennials and after a few years will begin to deteriorate and should be replaced. Start from seed in the fall or put out small plants in early spring. The seedlings need light to germinate, so do not cover them with soil. Once the flowers go to seed, the seed heads should be removed because columbines are subject to reversion. The seedlings do not stay true to the parent colors but generally produce an unattractive muddy-looking blossom. Columbines are often bothered by leaf miners, which create miniature roads in the leaves. This rarely does any real harm to the plant but often makes the foliage look a little ragged.

How to use: Columbines have traditionally been used in rock gardens or in the perennial border. The red-and-yellow species is sometimes difficult to include within a border because of its unusual color combination, but it looks wonderful planted among ferns or alongside white or yellow flowers.

Europeans are quite fond of columbines and use them prolifically in their gardens. Before the middle of the seventeenth century, the only species grown in Britain was *A. vulgaris*, though it had many different forms. Early American gardeners found different species of columbines growing in the wild in their new country and often included them in their cultivated gardens. John Tradescant sent one of these American columbines *(Aquilegia canadensis)* to England's Hampton Court in 1640.

Columbines were considered important medicinal plants during the Middle Ages. Along with seven other herbs, this plant was made into a concoction used to treat the "pestilence." Other medicinal claims include being a cure for liver ailments, measles, smallpox, sore throats, jaundice, and swollen glands. Care should be taken when using this plant, however, for it is a member of the *Ranunculaceae* (buttercup) family, many of which are considered poisonous.

The English herbalist John Gerard called columbine *Herba lionis*, in reference to the superstition that lions ate columbine in the spring to revive their strength.

Favorite old-fashioned varieties include Queen Charlotte (pink) and whirlwind (white).

Common name: CROCUS
Botanical name: *Crocus* sp.
Introduced: White, small purple, large purple, and yellow crocuses introduced to the colonies during the 1700s
Description: Many different species and cultivars of crocus are common in gardens today. In general, crocuses have cup-shaped flowers in shades of blue, purple, white, yellow, or pink. The foliage is grass-like. In some species the leaves appear before the blossoms; in others they appear together. The plants usually grow to a height of three to six inches. Some of the more outstanding species include: *C. biflorus, C. imperati* (blue), *C. chrysanthus* (yellow), *C. laevigatus* (white).

How to grow: Crocuses should be planted in the fall from corms buried to a depth of three to four inches. They like full sun and rich, well-drained soil. The plants will benefit from annual spring feedings. The foliage must be left to die back naturally (not cut) to allow the plant to produce its own food.

How to use: Because crocuses bloom so early in the gardening year, they are indispensable in the spring garden. Planted en masse, they make a spectacular show.

Several records indicate that crocuses are among the oldest of all cultivated plants. In *The English Gardener* Leonard Maeger says that a scroll dated 1552 lists medicinal uses for crocuses.

Crocuses were first reported as arriving in England in the sixteenth century. They were brought from the Mideast and created much excitement at the Elizabethan court.

The Greek word for thread, *krokos*, was the basis for the name crocus. It was used because of the thread-like stigmas of crocus. The herb saffron comes from the stigmas of *Crocus sativa* and has always been of enormous value. As late as 1983 the price of saffron was $4.59 for one-fortieth of an ounce. That translates to three thousand dollars per pound. Golden cloth dyed with saffron was worn by aristocrats in both Europe and the Orient. Saffron has also been used as medicine, in perfumes, and as a magical herb.

According to the Victorian language of flowers, the crocus is symbolic of youthful gladness, of mirth and laughter.

Common name: FRITILLARIA
Botanical name: *Frittilaria meleagris*
Introduced: Brought to U.S. in 1600s
Description: Fritillaria is seldom mistaken for anything else. The graceful, nodding blossoms are composed of pinkish-purple checkers. The leaves are long and narrow, and the plants grow to a height of about twelve inches, with a spread of six inches. This species blooms toward the end of April. Another species in this genus is *Frittilaria imperialis*. This imposing-looking plant bears as many as eight large red or yellow blossoms to a stem, which can grow to be three feet tall. Crown imperial, as it is often called, blooms for only about ten days at the end of May.

How to grow: Fritillarias are intolerant of wet soil, and for this reason are often included within a dry rock garden. They should be grown in very well-drained, sandy soil in full sun. Both species need half-day sun. Plant the bulbs in fall, four inches deep (for *F. meleagris*) or eight inches deep (*F. imperialis*).

How to use: *Frittilaria imperialis* can be difficult to use in the spring garden because it is so large it often overpowers everything else. A special place all to itself is perhaps best to show off its true beauty. *F. meleagris* is easier to use and looks wonderful in a naturalized setting with other small bulbs and ornamental grasses.

Frittilaria is dedicated to St. Edward, a tenth-century king and martyr murdered by his stepmother. The plant is said to bloom on his day, March 18.

The liquid found in the base of the flower is thought to have special

29

powers. A Persian legend says that a queen, unjustly doubted by her husband, cried many tears. An angel, full of compassion, turned her into a flower, but until the queen is reunited with her husband, the tears will remain and can be found at the base of frittilaria.

Although there are several frittilarias native to the western United States, the more commonly used garden varieties are native to Persia (now Iran) and are sometimes referred to as Persian lilies. The regal *Frittilaria imperialis*, or crown imperial, was first introduced to English gardeners in 1572 when it was brought to their country by Huguenots fleeing from France. The English became entranced with this lily-looking plant and often included it within their gardens in spite of its highly unpleasant odor. Rubbing the bulb will produce an odor similar to that of a fox den. This bulb, although supposedly cooked and eaten by the Persians, is poisonous if eaten raw.

Frittilaria meleagris, native to Great Britain, was also often used within formal gardens. This plant has a multitude of folk names drawn from the unique coloration of its petals. These include checkered lily, leopard lily, leper's lily, Lazarus bell, guinea hen flower, and checkered bell. Not all of its names have been complimentary. Because the flowers hang down, it was called sullen lady, drooping tulip, drooping young man, and ugly lady. Other common names were given because of the unusual formation of the buds: toad's head, snake flower, and turkey eggs.

Common name: GRAPE HYACINTH
Botanical name: *Muscari botryoides*
Introduced: Introduced to U.S. during the 1700s
Description: Grape hyacinths grow to a height of six to eight inches and produce spikes of rounded, almost closed blossoms. Foliage is linear and grass-like. The plants spread about three inches across. *M. botryoides* blooms early in spring. A related species, *M. armeniacum*, has leaves that appear in fall and flowers in spring.
How to grow: Grape hyacinth does best grown in rich, organic garden soil. It prefers full sun or partial shade. The small bulbs should be planted in fall three inches deep and three to four inches apart.
How to use: Because of the dark blue color of the blossoms, it is best to plant grape hyacinth against a backdrop of lighter color.

These small flowers, grown from bulbs, are native to southern Europe, northern Africa, and western Asia. The species *M. botryoides* is called starch hyacinth because the plant has a distinctly starch-like odor. The species name is from Greek and means "a bunch of grapes."

The genus name, *Muscari*, is also from Greek and means "musk," for many species within the genus produce a deeply sweet, musky scent.

Discorides, a Greek physician, wrote of the bulbs "of this wort it is said that it was produced out of dragon's blood, on top of mountains, in thick forests." Bulbs from some species were considered quite a delicacy when made into pickles.

Common name: HONESTY
Botanical name: *Lunaria annua*
Introduced: Introduced to colonial gardens between 1700 and 1776
Description: Honesty grows to be about thirty-six inches tall. The blossoms are small pinkish-purple flowers with four petals each. The leaves are large, toothed, and heart-shaped. The plant is more often grown for its interesting seed pods than its small flowers.
How to grow: *Lunaria* is very easy to grow and in some areas is even considered overly aggressive. Seeds from this annual should be sown outdoors in midspring or indoors four to six weeks before the last frost date. Soil needs to be rich and well drained. The plant does best in full sun but will tolerate light shade.
How to use: The seed pods are most unusual and lovely. Once they have matured, cut the branches and remove the outer covering from the pods. Then hang them upside down and allow to dry thoroughly.

The unusual seed pods gave rise to many different common names for this plant: honesty, silver penny, silver shilling, moneywort, money plant, money-in-the-pocket, pennyflower, money seed, white satin, satin seed, and satin pod.

The genus name, *Lunaria*, is from the Latin word for moon, for it was thought that the round silver seedpods looked like the moon.

Witches were said to use honesty for various spells and trances: to open locks, break chains, banish monsters and demons, and make witches fly faster on their brooms. According to the Victorian language of flowers, honesty is symbolic of honest emotions and fascination. It is used most often in dried arrangements, where it lasts several months without losing its charm.

Common name: IRIS
Botanical name: *Iris* sp.
Introduced: Many native irises used in colonial gardens during the 1600s; first imported irises: *Iris susiana* (mourning iris), *Iris variegata*, and *Iris xiphiodes*
Description: Bearded iris is composed of three petals that stand upright (standards), three petals that are pointed outward (falls), and beards on the falls. Foliage is long, linear, and grass-like. These iris are tall (thirty to thirty-six inches) and bloom in May and June.
How to grow: Bearded iris grows from rhizomes planted in fall. Rich,

Iris Germanica

IRIS.

(Rainbow Flower, Fleur de Lis.)

" The Orchid of the Flower Garden." The flowers of this family are the richest and most varied in color of any hardy garden plants, and for cut flowers they are invaluable. An almost continuous display of bloom can be kept up by planting the following varieties. When grown in pots or frames for winter blooming, commence with *Alata* and *Histrio*, which will bloom in December and January, then follow *Reticulata* in February, then *Bakeri*, after which those in the open ground will commence with *Bakeri* and *Pavonia* in April and May, followed by the *Spanish* in June, then the *English*, then *Germanica*, the last in bloom being the *Kæmpferi* in July and August.

fertile soil and plenty of sunshine are necessary components for successful growths. Irises need abundant moisture while blooming but can withstand long periods of drought during summer months. Apply a light fertilizer in spring and cut the plants back to within four or five inches of the rhizome in fall.

How to use: Irises make a spectacular late spring garden plant as well as being much sought after as cut flowers.

The iris is the basis for the French *fleur-de-lis*, the three-part flower found on the French flag. The connection between France and the iris dates back to the year 496 when Clovis I, an early French leader, was fighting an important battle. He found himself trapped between a lake and an opposing army. Legend says that Clovis knelt and prayed to God, asking Him for a sign of salvation. When he arose from his knees, Clovis saw a yellow flag iris growing midway across the lake and realized that it was not a lake, but a bog,

32

probably shallow enough to march his army across to safety. He did so, and when his men were out of danger, they picked iris blossoms and declared them symbols of salvation. In later years the three large petals of the iris became representative of faith, wisdom, and valor. Pliny, a Roman statesman, suggested that only the chaste of heart could successfully harvest iris.

Irises have been used as medicine and in cosmetics for thousands of years. Romans, Egyptians, and Moors used iris root to cure epilepsy, headaches, loose teeth, and the bite of a serpent. During the Middle Ages irises were grown in monastery gardens for their medicinal value. They were considered good for the "bite of a venomous beast and for sunburn," according to an early book on healing. The lovely scent of iris root has been used in the manufacturing of perfumes since early Greek days. Today in Mexico many acres of *I. florentina* are grown for the perfume industry.

Iris can sometimes be found growing on roofs in Japan. Early in Japanese history warlords forbade the general populace from growing flowers in their gardens. To bypass this law, the Japanese grew iris on the roofs of their houses instead. Another explanation for rooftop irises in Japan refers to the superstition that irises could keep away lightning with their electric blue flowers.

I. kaempferi was introduced to England in 1857. *I. unquicularis* was brought to England from the eastern Mediterranean and northern Africa in the late nineteenth century. *I. chrysographes* was introduced in 1911.

Common name: LILY OF THE VALLEY
Botanical name: *Convallaria majalis fortuneii*
Introduced: Used in colonial gardens before 1700
Description: Graceful arching stems hold small, bell-like white flowers. The leaves are large and deeply ribbed and clasp the stem. The plant blooms

in spring and grows to be eight to ten inches tall.

How to grow: Lily of the valley is considered easy to grow and should be planted in rich, well-drained soil in an area that receives light shade or well filtered sunlight. Top dress with fertilizer in fall, and the plants will remain healthy and spread easily.

How to use: Lily of the valley makes a charming groundcover. The leaves look good for many months after the plant blooms.

The Dutch believed that if newlyweds planted this plant in their first garden, the annual blooms would represent the renewed love of the couple. For this reason it was often carried in bridal bouquets. Called virgin's tears in Germany, lily of the valley was thought to be a sign of good luck. It is the national flower of Finland, and the French wear a sprig in their lapels on May Day.

An English legend dates its origins back to medieval times, when Saint Leonard fought a ferocious dragon and much blood was spilled. Wherever the saint lost a drop of blood, lily of the valley began to grow. Wherever the dragon lost blood, thorns and weeds began to grow.

Lily of the valley has been considered a symbol of purity and humility, sweetness and renewed happiness. In some parts of the world, it has been believed to have the power to help men envision a better world.

Lily of the valley was often used for medicinal purposes as well. It was thought to cure gout and, if mixed with wine and spread on the forehead and neck, to give people common sense. In spite of its reputed value as medicine, all parts of the plant are poisonous and should not be eaten.

Common name: NARCISSUS

Botanical name: *Narcissus* sp.

Introduced: Many species grown in gardens in this country in the 1600s

Description: Although there are only twenty-six species in this genus, there are hundreds of cultivars which have their own personalities. A daffodil is a narcissus with a center trumpet that is longer or as long as the surrounding petals. Daffodils bloom only one flower to a stem. Other kinds of narcissi have shallower center trumpets or cups. Jonquils come in clusters of blossoms, each with a shallow cup whose color contrasts with the petals. Most narcissi are perennials and bloom in spring.

How to grow: Narcissi are among the easiest spring plants to grow. Bulbs should be planted in fall in an area that receives full or half-day sun. They like rich, well-drained soil. After the plants bloom, remove the faded flower heads and allow the foliage to die back naturally. To cut it robs the plant of essential food for the next year.

Wild daffodils grew in great profusion in Great Britain and were dearly beloved by country folk there. The first Sunday in April was considered "Daffodil Sunday," and people would flock to the fields to pick blossoms to take to the hospitals and wards in London. Soon this practice began to deplete the plant's native population. Corrective measures were taken to ensure their survival.

The name daffodil probably came from an old English word, *affodyle*, meaning "that which comes early," referring to the time of its bloom. The name jonquil comes from the native Spanish narcissus, *juncas*, meaning "rush," because jonquil leaves are similar to those of rush.

The legend about the origin of narcissus comes from Greek mythology. A young nymph named Echo fell in love with Narcissus, a vain youth interested only in his own beauty. Narcissus spent all day every day staring at his reflection in a pool of water and simply ignored Echo's love. Finally she faded away; only her voice remained. This so angered the gods that they changed Narcissus into a flower, destined always to sit by the pool and nod at its reflection.

The daffodil is the floral emblem of the Chinese New Year.

Superstition in the state of Maine says that if you point at a daffodil

with your finger, you will cause it not to bloom.

Narcissus poeticus is first mentioned in histories around 320 B.C. and is thought to have been introduced to England at a very early date as well. Many forms have been developed, including *recurvus*, sometimes called "Old Pheasant's Eye." By the eighteenth century *N. magalis* was naturalized in England and was often included in Victorian gardens.

Common name: PANSY
Botanical name: *Viola wittrockiana*
Introduced: Viola tricolor, Johnny-jump-up used in colonial gardens during the 1700s, native violets, during the 1600s
Description: Pansies are just grown-up violets. There are many flowers to each plant, each borne on a separate stem. The blossoms are either all the same color or the three lower petals show a different color than the top two. New hybrid strains have resulted in enormous flower sizes, sometimes as large as four inches across.
How to grow: Pansies need cool weather, as they become leggy and unattractive with increased temperatures. In mild regions, sow pansy seeds in late summer or set out plants in early fall. In colder areas, sow seeds indoors during January or February.
How to use: In a mass planting, pansies make a real springtime show.

Pansies have always been associated with love, a fact to which their multitude of common names alludes. Tickle-my-fancy, kiss-her-in-the-pantry, heartsease, and cull-me-to-you are all names for pansy. According to Christian legend, the three large petals of pansies represent the doctrine of the Trinity.

The Celts made a love potion from dried pansy leaves. According to the doctrine of signatures, which suggests that a plant will be useful in curing whatever it physically resembles, heart-shaped pansy leaves could cure heartaches.

Pansy is from the French word *pense*, which means "thought." The name, given to this plant years ago, reflects the belief that pansies can make your lover think of you. The three original pansy colors—purple, white, and yellow—were thought to symbolize loving thoughts, memories, and souvenirs, all of which ease the hearts of separated lovers.

According to an ancient legend, all pansies used to be white and gained the purple and yellow colors only when they were pierced by Cupid's arrow.

German and Scottish folktales explain why pansies have been called "stepmother": the large lower petal being the mother, the two large petals to either side being the well-dressed daughters, and the two small upper petals the poor stepdaughters.

Common name: PEONY
Botanical name: *Paeonia officinalis*
Introduced: Grown in colonial gardens during the seventeenth century
Description: Large, beautiful red, pink, or white flowers are borne on shrubby two- to four-foot plants. The blossoms can be single, semidouble, or double and are all of exquisite beauty, measuring three to four inches across.
How to grow: Peonies are particularly long-lived plants, some specimens being as old as one hundred years. Peonies do not transplant well and should not be moved once they are established. They like neutral or slightly alkaline soils, high in fertility and rich in organic matter. The roots should be planted so that the eyes are one-and-one-half inches below the soil level. Where summers are hot, a bit of shade protects the plants.
How to use: Peony blossoms are relatively short-lived, but the foliage stays attractive throughout the summer months. Peonies make a wonderful foundation plant for the perennial border.

Old-Fashioned Peony

Peonies are named for Paeon, physician to the Greek gods and a student of Asclepius (god of medicine and healing). Paeon was told about a magical root growing on Mount Olympus that could soothe the pain of women in childbirth. Paeon obtained this root, and Asclepius became so jealous and angry he threatened to kill his pupil. Paeon was saved by Leto, goddess of fertility, who changed him into the peony.

For many centuries peony seeds were given to pregnant women to help soothe their pains. Other medicinal uses were to cure insanity, prevent epileptic convulsions, and sooth the gums of teething infants. Peonies, called the blessed herb, were used as protection against witchcraft, demons, and nightmares. Peony seeds were strung around an infant's neck as protection against the "evil eye."

Records from the Philadelphia Centennial Exposition in 1876 show that peony plants had been cultivated and enjoyed in this country since colonial days. Some of the more popular old-fashioned varieties include Therese, Duchess of Teck, and Eugene Verdier, all of which had pink double flowers. Of the single-flowering varieties, Flamboyant, Gypsy, and Queen Alexandra were considered the best.

At one time peonies were considered symbolic of the American spirit of ambition and determination to adapt and thrive.

Buttercup

Common name: PINKS

Botanical Name: *Dianthus* sp.

Introduced: Called clove gilliflowers or pinks, red-and-white and pink-and-white pinks grown in colonial gardens during the seventeenth century; *D. caryophyllus* (carnations) and *D. plumarius* (grass pinks or cottage pinks) introduced between 1700 and 1776

Description: Pinks include many species of low-growing, sweet-smelling perennials. The blossoms are usually white, pink, or red; the foliage, small, linear, and grey-green. In mild climates this foliage is evergreen. Mostly perennial, pinks bloom in late spring to early summer. Sweet William (*D. barbatus*) has dense heads of fragrant blossoms on twenty-four-inch stems. This is usually grown as a biennial. Maiden pink (*D. deltoides*) has red or pink flowers with dark red centers. It grows in dense mounds and reaches a height of twelve inches. Border pink (*D. plumarius*) is also known as cottage pink, Scotch pink, and grass pink. The blossoms measure one-and-one-half inches across and the plant grows to be twelve to fifteen inches high.

How to grow: Pinks like full sun and well-drained, slightly alkaline soil. They do best in relatively cool weather. Keep faded flowers picked to prolong the blooming period. Plants should be spaced twelve to eighteen inches apart and should be divided every three years.

How to use: Because they are low-growing and have a neat growth habit, pinks make a wonderful edging plant. Some of the smaller varieties can be used quite effectively in the rock garden. They can also be used as a ground cover in a small, sunny area.

The name pinks was given to this genus not because of its color, but because the word *pink* also means to cut with a jagged edge, as you would with pinking shears. Because the petal edges of this genus are jagged, this group of plants was nicknamed pinks.

Although pinks are quite lovely and add great beauty to the flower border, their spicy, sweet fragrance first intrigued early gardeners.

Evidence shows that pinks have been cultivated since at least the 1450s, for drawings of carnations have been found on tiles dating back to that time. During Roman times, carnations became the symbol of high civilization. The genus name, *Dianthus*, means "divine flower," and the flowers were called *flos Jovis*, or Jove's flower. During the Renaissance, pinks were symbolic of carefree happiness and, according to an ancient herbal, were used to "treat melancholy and cheer the heart."

Old-fashioned gardeners often used pinks as flavoring. The petals can be chopped and added to batter for muffins or bread. They give a distinct sweet and spicy flavor to any recipe.

In 1835 *Horticulture* magazine described *Dianthus*: "Sometimes a cultivator is fortunate enough to raise one with rose-leaved edges; but it is rare and thought much of. The fringed petals are not considered detrimental to the pink, provided the indentations are small and regular, not jagged; but the great beauty of this flower depends on the distinctness and brilliancy of the color round the edge of the petals called the lacing."

Common name: PRIMROSE
Botanical Name: *Primula polyanthus*
Introduced: Introduced to colonial gardens before 1700
Description: Low-growing plants, primroses have clusters of flat blossoms, each with five petals. Blossoms come in all colors including purple, red, pink, gold, and white. Each has a small yellow eye. The leaves are thick and crinkly and are all basal.
How to grow: Primroses need rich, moist, well-drained soil. They do best if grown in light shade. Plants can be set out in fall or spring and should be spaced twelve inches apart. They are short-lived perennials and should be replaced every few years.
How to use: Because they do well in the shade, primroses can be included within a woodland garden along with plants such as astilbe and ferns.

According to a German legend, primroses first came to earth when St. Peter found some not-so-ready souls trying to sneak into the back gate of heaven. He was so upset he dropped the keys to the Pearly Gate, and where they fell the primrose began to grow. Nicknames suggest this connection with keys: Our Lady's key, marriage key, the key flower, virgin's keys and Saint Peter's keys. Superstition suggests that primroses can be used to open treasure chests.

To "walk down the primrose path" means to lead a life of pleasure and self-indulgence, reflecting another of the primrose's symbolic meanings: wantonness.

The primrose held great magical and some medicinal value as well. It was used to restore lost speech and to combat vertigo and cure convulsions, hysteria, and neck and muscular spasms, to say nothing of its supposed power to cure the bite of mad dogs.

The plant was once in great demand as a beauty aid. An ointment made from the blossoms was used to remove spots and wrinkles from the face. The rough leaves were also rubbed on the cheeks to produce a rosy glow.

The English have always been particularly fond of primroses. Buckner Hollingsworth said in his book *Flower Chronicles*, "England displays a rose on the royal coat of arms, but she carries a primrose in her heart."

During the early seventeenth century striped primroses were all the rage. By the end of this century yellow varieties were scorned as being too common and were replaced in popularity by reds, crimsons, and purples. About this time primroses were first grown in pots, often creating fantastic displays as pot after pot of blooming plants were put on stage. During the 1880s April 19 was declared Primrose Day in England. According to the English floral calendar, however, the primrose is the flower for February.

Common name: SCILLA
Botanical name: *Scilla siberica*
Introduced: Introduced to the U.S. between 1700 and 1776
Description: Scilla blooms early in spring and has four- to six-inch spikes of deep blue bell-shaped blossoms measuring one-half inch across. The foliage is long, linear, and grass-like.
How to grow: Scilla needs rich, well-drained soil and either full sun or partial shade. The small bulbs should be planted in fall about four inches deep. Mulch in fall with well-rotted manure or compost. This bulb has been extensively collected in the wild. When purchasing, make sure that you are dealing with a reputable firm that has propagated the plant for sale. Do not buy plants that have been dug from the wild.
How to use: Scilla multiplies rapidly and makes a wonderful spring blooming ground cover for a naturalized setting.

During the sixteenth and seventeenth centuries, scilla was extremely popular and many species and varieties were grown. Today the plant seems to have lost some of its popularity.

The word *scilla* means "to dry," as to dry up humors in the body. The "syrup of squills," made from scilla, was a medicinal concoction used to treat patients with heart disease. The plant also provides the substance used to make a deadly and widely used rat poison. Bulbs from the plant give forth a substance that was used as starch for stiffening collars during Elizabethan times.

The Welsh call scilla cuckoo's boots.

Common name: SWEET PEA
Botanical name: *Lathyrus odoratus*
Introduced: Grown in colonial gardens during the 1600s
Description: Old-fashioned sweet pea has a sweet, lingering fragrance. Pea-like flowers come in shades of purple, red, white, pink, or blue and are borne either on trailing vines or bushy, two-and-one-half-foot-tall plants.
How to grow: Sweet peas need rich, well-drained soil and full sun. They should be watered frequently during hot, dry summer months. Seeds for this annual should be sown outdoors early in spring. Work the planting bed well, adding plenty of organic matter and enough lime to make it slightly alkaline.
How to use: Trailing varieties can be beautifully grown if trained on a trellis

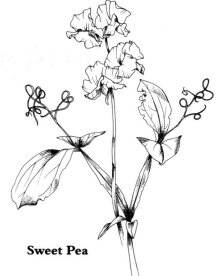

Sweet Pea

40

or fence. The old-fashioned varieties have a scent superior to the newer hybrids.

The only thing going for the original sweet pea was its fabulous odor. The plant itself, six feet tall, weak stemmed, and small flowered, was first found growing in fields in Sicily. Plant breeders worked with it, breeding and crossbreeding until they developed the lovely garden flower we enjoy today.

During Edwardian England sweet peas were so popular that many gardeners considered them the emblem of England. In 1900 a bicentennial where more than 250 varieties of sweet peas were displayed was staged. Reverend W. T. Hutchins said of sweet pea that it had "a fragrance like the universal gospel, yea, a sweet prophecy of welcome everywhere that has been abundantly fulfilled."

Superstition suggests that, to get the most beautiful blossoms possible, you must sow sweet pea seeds before sunrise on Saint Patrick's Day.

Sweet pea is April's emblem on the English floral calendar. In America some of the favorite garden varieties include Lavender King, Princess, Blue Bird, Zephyr, Gypsy Maid, Fairy, Cheerful, Peach Blossom, Flamingo, Fairy Queen, and Fire King.

Common name: THRIFT
Botanical name: *Armeria maritima* var. *elongata*
Introduced: Introduced to the U.S. between 1850 and 1900
Description: Thrift is a low-growing perennial with evergreen, grass-like foliage. The small globe-shaped flower clusters are purplish pink, pink, or sometimes white. They appear in spring.
How to grow: Thrift grows well in average garden soil. If the soil is too rich, the plant will not bloom. The plant prefers sandy, well-drained soil and full sun. The clumps eventually die out in the center and need to be rejuvenated by division and replanting every three to four years. New plants should be spaced nine to twelve inches apart.
How to use: Traditionally, thrift has been used between paving stones or in rock wall gardens. It can also be used in the front of a border.

Thrift has had several names and was very popular with English gardeners. Also known as ladies' cushion (from Elizabethan times) and sea pink (because it grows so well in coastal gardens), thrift has been known and loved for many years.

Some species of *Armeria* actually make neat, low-growing shrubs and can be used to make patterns in knot gardens. During the mid-1800s some of the most popular garden species included *Armeria laucheana* (which resembled miniature carnations) and *Armeria latifolia* (also known as *A. pseudoarmeria*).

Common name: TULIP
Botanical name: *Tulipa* sp.
Introduced: Single and double varieties grown in colonial gardens in the 1600s
Description: There is tremendous variety within the genus *Tulipa*, but almost all have flowers with three petals and three petal-like sepals, all of which are identical. Leaves are generally borne at the base of the plant but sometimes along the flowering stem as well. Blossoms come in almost every

color except true blue. There are thousands of tulip hybrids and between fifty and 150 species.

How to grow: Tulips grow from a bulb that should be planted two to four inches deep in fall. They perform best in full sun or partial shade in rich, well-drained, sandy soil. Tulips need good cold weather. In mild regions they will not bloom well after the first year and are often treated as annual bulbs.

How to use: Because of the bold, clean colors of tulips, they are a must for a showy spring garden.

Tulipmania is a phenomenon unique in the history of flowers. Holland in 1634 was the scene for wild enthusiasm over these flowers, and the price of bulbs was often more than that of precious metals. A single bulb of the variety Semper Augustus is said to have sold for fifty-five hundred florins, equivalent to twenty-five hundred dollars today.

Tulipmania did not have a happy ending, however, for many Dutch farmers, hoping to make quick money, planted fields of tulip bulbs instead of food. When the market for bulbs crashed, these farmers were left destitute.

Designs on pottery jars dating back to 1600 B.C. show tulip designs, indicating that the flowers have been cultivated for many centuries. They were first found by European explorers and traders growing in Turkish gardens in the early 1500s. In Europe they were first grown in Austria and later in the Netherlands, where they flourished and soon became an important export. Dutch colonists first brought tulip bulbs to America. Their impact can be determined by the prevalence of tulips in Pennsylvania Dutch designs.

According to the Victorian langauge of flowers, tulips are a sign of perfect love. Red petals mean a declaration of love; yellow, hopeless love; and variegated petals, beautiful eyes.

Common name: VINCA
Botanical name: *Vinca minor*
Introduced: Introduced to this country in the early 1700s
Description: Perennial vinca has light blue flowers and grows on a fast-spreading vine. The leaves are narrow and oblong, shiny and evergreen. The popular bedding plant called vinca is actually *Catharanthus roseus* and has attractive white-and-pink or red flowers. It grows to a height of ten to fifteen inches.
How to grow: Vinca grows just fine in sun or shade. It can be propagated in spring by replanting sprigs taken from established plants.
How to use: Vinca makes an outstanding ground cover, though it can be an aggressive vine and care should be taken to control it properly.

If placed over the doorway, vinca was thought to have the power to keep away witches. In Belgium it was a symbol of virginity, and petals from the flowers were spread in front of bridal couples as they left the church.

If planted outside the garden gate, red vinca was considered an invitation for all passersby to come and visit in the garden.

Roots of the vinca plant were used to prevent nightmares and to soothe nerves and hysteria. If eaten daily, vinca was thought to bring about a happy, comfortable life. Its evergreen leaves symbolize friendship and fidelity, and the blue-and-white blossoms are emblems of the pleasures of memory while the red blossoms mean early friendship.

Common name: WALLFLOWER
Botanical name: *Cheiranthus cheiri*
Introduced: Unknown
Description: Yellow, orange, and apricot-colored blossoms emit a delicious odor in late spring when wallflower is in bloom. The one-inch blossoms are found in showy clusters. The plant grows to a height of twelve to thirty inches.
How to grow: Wallflower likes bright full sun and average-to-rich garden soil. Seeds can be sown in an outdoor planting bed six to eight weeks before they will be transplanted. Plants should be spaced twelve to fifteen inches apart.
How to use: Wallflower looks very good in a wildflower or naturalized planting. The bright yellow or orange blossoms are good to bring indoors because of their sweet fragrance.

Historical uses of wallflower are quite varied. A distillation of wallflower was thought good for fertility problems. Drunk twice a day for three to four weeks, this water was believed to make women fruitful. The sweet scent of the flower gave rise to the genus name, *Cheiranthus*, from two Greek words meaning "hand" and "flower" because the flowers were often carried in bouquets to overpower the stench of the streets. During the Middle Ages wallflower was worn by troubadours as a sign of good luck. It was considered a symbol of faithfulness in adversity. One of the most popular Victorian varieties was the Negress, which was the deep, rich color of a ripe mulberry.

SUMMER

My grandma and grandpa's farmhouse in Kentucky had the most wonderful front porch in the world: big, wide, furnished with the essential porch swing, and decorated with Grandma's prized potted plants. This porch was much more than an extension of the house. It was a magically cool haven from the heat of the late afternoon sun. One by one, as we finished the day's chores or activities, we would find our way to the front porch.

Sinking down into the swing or an empty rocking chair, we would simply sit and let the cool of the porch soothe our sun-wearied bodies. Grandma, who in those days never seemed to quit working or get tired, would bring out an old black tray full of glasses of lemonade.

And there we would sit, lazily chatting until it was time to go in to help with supper. After supper, once the dishes were washed, we'd end up back the porch. Then the real magic of the evening would begin.

Grandma always had a moonvine plant growing up the sides of the porch. She tied support strings from the roof down to the railing, and by midsummer its big leaves covered the strings and created a wall of lush green. Just at that mystical moment when sunlight turns

to darkness, the dance of the moonvine began. Plump buds began to quiver with excitement, and we all watched, fascinated, as they began to open one by one. It was like watching high-speed photography, for in a matter of five minutes, buds became fully opened, beautiful white flowers.

The front porch was an important part of our family life, the stage for courtship and conversation, for greeting neighbors and displaying the best, brightest, and most unusual flowers that Grandma could lay her hands on.

During the summer months the porch was home to all the parlor plants. Those housebound beauties reveled in their freedom and stretched their roots and branches until they fairly burst out of their

pots. But the real glory of the porch was the summer annuals that Grandma planted with care and displayed with pride. Some plants she always had: a hanging basket full of pink and purple fuschias, a big iron pot of red geraniums, and, during the summer months, a procession of beauties that included begonias, lantanas, ageratum, lobelia, petunias, and marigolds.

But Grandma also used her porch to show off some really strange and curious plants. Every year she would indulge in ordering seeds of some exotic plant. We saw geraniums scented like pineapples, voodoo lilies, sensational amaryllis, and huge hibiscus. Some years her exotics would not even come up from seed, but we refrained from asking what had happened. Other years Grandma would have better luck, and the porch looked like an African rain forest.

While the front porch was used for entertaining and for casual family gatherings, the back porch was for work. Next to the kitchen, the back porch provided a great place for soaking seeds before planting and for hardening off seedlings before putting them into the ground. During harvest, it was an ideal place to peel apples, shuck corn, and shell peas.

I suppose that if I had to choose one favorite place in all the world from any time period, from any location I wanted, that place would be Grandma's front-porch swing. There I was not tied to reality. There I could close my eyes and be anyone and anything I wanted. There, on Grandma's front-porch swing, anything was possible.

OLD ROSES

Next to my grandma, Mrs. Eubanks was the best gardener I knew. She was a beautiful little old lady with snow-white hair and a face wrinkled by time and laughter. Through the years she seemed to grow smaller and smaller, until finally she was just a tiny wisp of a person. But she could grow the most beautiful roses in the entire world.

Mrs. Eubanks lived right around the corner from us in the outskirts of Atlanta and was a friend of my mother's. I remember distinctly the first time I went to visit her garden. My mother was preparing for a party and had called Mrs. Eubanks to ask if she could have a few roses for decoration. Mrs. Eubanks, forever generous, said to come on over. I was amazed. I'd never known anyone with enough roses to give them away. When we got there, I was even more amazed, for there were roses everywhere of all colors and every fragrance.

I walked to the middle of the garden and stood still, drinking in their beauty.

Mrs. Eubanks walked up to me. "They're lovely, aren't they?" She took my arm and said, "Come on, I'll introduce you." We strolled down the center walkway. At each rose she stopped to cup it lovingly in her hand and tell me about it.

She introduced me to the Peace rose and told me the story of how it was brought into the nursery trade after World War II. I met Queen Elizabeth with her clear pink flowers, and Celsiana, a rose that has been grown for many, many years. I met roses Mrs. Eubanks had grown for thirty-six years, and newcomers she had planted only that year. She knew each by name and cared for each as she would a child.

"Where did they all come from?" I finally asked.

Mrs. Eubanks smiled; her eyes filled with tears. "When I met Mr. Eubanks and we fell in love, he told me that he couldn't promise that we would be wealthy and he couldn't promise that we'd never have trouble, but he could promise me a rose garden. Well, we certainly were never rich, and we had our times of trouble just like everybody else. But he did keep his promise. He did give me a rose garden.

"He died twelve years ago this past May. The times that I miss him the most are when I'm working in this garden. He used to love to come out here and just piddle around, knocking bugs off the plants or keeping the weeds out. I know that these flowers meant the world to him, and even though it makes me sad to be here without him, I've got lovely memories of our times together in the rose garden."

The lure of growing roses is almost irresistible to anyone who digs in the dirt. James Horace McFarland, an early twentieth-century gardener and writer, said that he would love to plant a rose hedge all around his property but that he was "word-persuaded and pocket-convinced" that this was not practical. To the old-fashioned gardener, nothing can surpass the simple elegance and beauty of the old roses. There is some question, however, just what constitutes "old." A conversation overheard at a garden club meeting illustrates this fact:

> *"What do you call old?"*
>
> *"Old roses are those of the type and class used in good gardens of the past."*
>
> *"Oh, and when did the past end?"*

Perhaps a more precise definition of an "old rose" is that these are roses grown before the introduction of the first hybrid tea rose in 1867.

The history of the rose is an ancient story filled with myth and magic. Roses were cultivated in many different ancient civilizations, including China, western Asia, and northern Africa. In the days of the Roman empire, roses were grown and used extravagantly. They soon became synonymous with wine and debauchery and were thus shunned by early Christian churches. During the medieval period,

Perle des Jardins

No other friends are so generous as dirt-gardener friends, and among these none are more generous than the friends of our neighborhood who grow and care for their own roses, old or new. Visit one of them and you are quite sure to be offered a cuttin'. —*Ethelyn Emery Keays,* Old Roses

however, roses were grown extensively in monastery gardens for their medicinal value and for their petals, which were used to create rosaries. The oldest known living rose bush, reportedly one thousand years old, is found at Hildesheim Cathedral in Germany.

The history of rose cultivation can be divided into three distinct periods. The first, the Colonial Period, extended from the first cultivation of roses until 1789. The second, the Federal Period, lasted from 1789 until 1840. The third, called the Great Forty Years, occurred from 1840 to 1880. During the early 1800s most of the roses grown in America came from either England or France. Nurserymen in our country boasted that a new breed of rose would be no older than one year before it was grown in America as well.

COLONIAL PERIOD—Roses grown during this period were characterized by their June bloom. The exceptions are a small group of damask roses that bloom more than once and the musk rose, which blooms early and lasts until frost. Outstanding roses dominant in this period include the gallica, cabbage, and moss roses.

The gallica rose, also called apothecary's rose, grows on a three-foot bush and blooms at the ends and from side shoots. The flower is large and semi-double with rose-red petals. When it was introduced, it exerted tremendous influence on rose growers throughout the world.

The cabbage rose, also called Provence, grows prolifically in the south of France. It is considered a must for old rose fanciers, who love its sweet fragrance and petals of lovely color, usually pink but sometimes shades of white or even purple.

The new roses are for admiring, the old ones for loving. — *Will Tillotson, founder, Roses of Yesterday and Today*

The moss rose takes its name from the resinous and glandulous mossiness of its sepals, calyx, and stem. It was introduced to England from Holland as early as 1596. In the *Rose Amateur's Guide* Thomas Rivers wrote, "What can be more elegant than the bud of the moss rose, with its pure rose colour, peeping through that beautiful and unique envelope?"

FEDERAL PERIOD — After 1789 scientists began experimenting with plant breeding, and the world of horticulture changed forever. Growing roses became quite the fashion, due in part to Empress Josephine and her incomparable rose collection at Malmaison. Great competition developed between England and France for developing new rose breeds. It was a time of trial and error, of experimentation. Everyone seemed anxious to try out ideas about the perfect rose.

Dominant roses during this period each had characteristics which endeared them to the breeder. Damask roses had a distinct perfume and could be relied on to bloom during June. China roses were everblooming; tea roses were sweetly scented. Semperflorens were a shade of red not seen before, which influenced the color of roses thereafter. Bourbons had fine outlines and clear, bright colors. The little noisettes were free blooming and had great clusters.

Breeders always considered the older roses. As one breeder put it, "It would indeed be unjust to neglect a good friend with sterling qualities."

GREAT FORTY YEARS — During this period the hybrid perpetuals ruled the rose world. Developed into an impressive strain of incomparable beauty, almost all of them had a truly lovely perfume as well. As one rose lover says, a hybrid perpetual is like Moses's serpent: it swallows up all the rest.

52

In 1931 Francis E. Lester wrote in the *American Rose Annual* that "The discovery, protection and preservation of our old roses constitutes a challenge to all rose lovers," a challenge rose lovers have taken to heart. Tremendous energy and effort is exerted to save the roses of former generations.

If you are interested in old roses, take every opportunity to include rare older species in your garden. If you can obtain only a part of a bush, or just a cutting, be diligent in propagating these varieties, particularly if you don't know anyone else growing them. While a rose is in bloom, take notes about its growth habit, the environmental

conditions that best suit it, when and how it blooms, and any other information that might be useful to someone else interested in growing that particular variety. Old roses fit in almost any garden. The tremendous variety within the realm of antique roses makes blending them with other flowers easy. Dwarf noisettes and tiny-flowered polyanthas can create hedges. A sweetbrier rose hedge can reach a height of five feet.

Old roses are not only beautiful but also relatively easy to grow because they are less susceptible to pests and disease, a fact Lewis Brabham, a gardener from South Carolina, has learned first hand.

"I'm age seventy-four, a retired *Greenville News* editor. In 1910, five years before my birth, a sister of mine, Lillie Sue Brabham, died at age seven. Several months after the death of my sister, a brother of my father planted a rose bush at the head of Lillie Sue's grave. No one, to my knowledge, during my adult lifetime has ever fertilized, sprayed or watered the rose bush. Yet, it is still living and blooming.

"In Greenville I have some three dozen rose bushes, and they require a lot of my time. Unless I pamper them, the bushes in my rose garden wouldn't do well and might even die. Yet the old-timey rose, set out nearly ninety years ago, is still living and producing roses."

Perhaps of all the stories and legends of roses, none is more touching than the true story of the Peace rose. Antoine Meillard, a French rose breeder in the early twentieth century, was known for the unique beauty of his roses. When Meillard was called to fight in World War I, he left his wife and young son to care for his roses. His wife had to work hard to grow enough to eat, but she also worked diligently to keep the roses alive. When the war was over, Meillard returned home to find much of his rose collection gone, but a few strains were still healthy and hardy. The entire family set to caring for, crossing, and cataloging these roses. In 1939 they were very proud of a new hybrid they had produced. A special showing of this new plant earned rave reviews, including one from the Duke of Windsor who pronounced it the most beautiful rose in the world.

When again Europe was threatened with war, the Meillards sent their new hybrid to safety: some to Germany, Italy, and the United States. At the end of World War II, rose breeders in all three of these countries were singing the praises of the Meillards' new rose. In Germany they called it Glory to God, in Italy, Joy; and in America, the most appropriate name of all, Peace. On April 29, 1945, the day Berlin fell, the new rose was officially named Peace.

Today, Peace is more widely grown than any other rose.

Roses

Tea Roses

Although many major mail order nurseries carry old-fashioned roses, several smaller nurseries specialize in old roses. Among them are:

Roses of Yesterday and Today
802 Brown's Valley Road
Watsonville, CA 95076-0398
Catalog $2.00

Pickering Nurseries
670 Kingston Road
Pickering, Ontario
Canada L1V 1A6
Catalog $2.00

Historical Roses
1657 West Jackson Street
Painesville, OH 44877
Catalog $1.00

Dr. Henry Najat
Heritage Roses Group
6365 Wald Road
Monroe, WI 53566
Membership $5.00

High Country Rosarium
1717 Downing Street
Denver, CO 80218
Catalog $1.00

Antique Rose Emporium
Route 5 Box 143
Brenham, TX 77833

Lowe's Own-Root Roses
6 Sheffield Road
Nashua, NH 03062
Catalog $2.00

Heritage Rose Gardens
16831 Mitchell Creek Drive
Fort Bragg, CA 95437
Catalog $1.00

GARDEN CRAFTS

Grandma was a regular and enthusiastic member of First Methodist Church in Louisville, Kentucky. Every week, come rain or shine, good health or bad, Grandma and Grandpa got into their old Ford station wagon and drove into town to go to church. Church was the center of Grandma's social life. Because they lived out in the country, she rarely got to visit with anyone except her closest neighbors, and she looked forward to Sunday mornings with real joy.

Part of her enthusiasm about church centered around arranging flowers for the church altar every Sunday. Grandma shared this enjoyable task with several other ladies, so when it was her week to arrange the church flowers, the entire household would be in a tizzy. Grandma would start practicing on Monday, snipping and clipping

this flower and that until she had a table full of floral beauties to choose from. She never picked her best specimens at this point. They were saved for the main event. During the week she picked just enough for trial runs. During this week Grandma would often forget

The Ladies are much inclined to have fine Flowers all summer long, about or upon the Chimneys, upon a Table or before a Window, either because of their beauty or because of their sweet Scent. — *Peter Kalm, Swedish naturalist and author of Travels in America (1850)*

to fix supper, the telephone remained unanswered, and all but the essential chores were ignored or forgotten.

The altar flowers were a solemn responsibility to my grandmother. She was stoic in the face of any almost any disaster, but I saw her reduced to tears when her prized peony (around which she had planned an entire arrangement) was beaten down and ruined by a late spring thunderstorm. I could never figure out what all the worry and fuss was about. Each and every one of Grandma's arrangements, the practice ones and the main event, were creations of great beauty. Grandma had a magic touch, and when divinely inspired, her arrangements were a glory to behold.

Cut Flowers and Flowers for the Church

Church arrangements in America in the nineteenth century were stiff and strongly geometric. They included a variety of blossoms such as aster, Canterbury bell, chrysanthemum, cornflower, forget-me-not, hyacinth, stock, sweet William, and tulip. Victorian England had great influence on floral decoration in this country. During this period, the arrangments in churches were massive and overstuffed, using ornate containers and flowers such as cockscomb, dahlias, foxglove, lilac, magnolia, and mignonette.

All evidence indicates that the average eighteenth-century housewife wanted to show off her flowers rather than display her skill in arranging them. At a time when interest in plant exploration and botany ran high, people would naturally on occasion have been proud of a single bloom and would have brought it indoors to display it.

Floral arrangements in early American homes depended upon geography (and therefore the type of flowers available), the affluence of the household, and the size and kind of house. Expansive Southern mansions needed much larger arrangements than did New England cottages. Early floral arrangements in New England were often simple mixed bouquets featuring contrasting, rather than harmonious, colors, often presented in pewter mugs and tankards.

Fragrance from indoor flowers was an important function of these early arrangements. During a time of infrequent bathing and relaxed sanitation practices, a sweetly scented arrangement did a great deal to dispel more unpleasant odors.

Like today's floral arranger, the colonial housewife had to condition flowers and foliage properly before putting them into an arrangement. The following suggestions can help in getting the most from the flowers you bring indoors:

Artemisia — Dip stems in boiling water for twenty seconds then leave in warm water for two hours.

Aster — Cut when three-quarters open and soak overnight in sugar solution.

Bleeding heart — Dip stem ends into boiling water for ten seconds then leave in cool water three hours or more.

Campanula — Place stem ends in boiling water for twenty seconds, then plunge in deep, cool water for three hours.

Chrysanthemum — Cut in full bloom, remove lower foliage, hammer ends of stems, and place in water to their necks for three hours.

Clematis — Crush stem ends lightly, take lower leaves off, and allow them a long drink before arranging.

Coreopsis — Cut blooms when fully open and place overnight in saline solution.

Cosmos — Cut blooms when almost open and leave them in cool water overnight.

Dahlia — Dip stems in boiling water for twenty seconds and let stand in sugar solution plus one aspirin.

Delphinium — Cut blooms when tops are still in bud, fill stem with weak starch solution, and plug end with a piece of cotton.

Gladiolus — Cut when buds begin to show color and set in cool water until ready to use.

Iris — Give a long drink before arranging.

Lily — Handle gently, for they bruise easily. Cut stems on a slant and place in warm water for several hours.

Marigold — Scrape bottom of stem to expose inner tissue and remove foliage beneath water level.

Narcissus — Cut as buds show color, wiping off sap before putting stems in water, and arrange in shallow water.

Phlox — Cut when clusters are half-open, split stems, and soak overnight in cool water.

Pinks, carnation — Cut stems at an angle between joints, put in water immediately, then cut when centers are tight and outer petals are firm.

Peony — Cut when petals begin to open and put in warm water.

Poppy — Cut before fully open, dip stems in boiling water for twenty seconds, then place in cool water for several hours.

Primroses — Prick stems under flower head and plunge into warm water.

Rose — Cut as buds begin to open and hammer stems.
Sweet pea — Handling as little as possible, arrange in shallow water.
Tulip — Cut off white part of stem, wrap stems together in bunches in newspaper, place in a warm, weak starch solution, and prick stems just under flower head with a pin.
Zinnia — Cut right above a leaf joint, remove extra foliage, place ends in boiling water for twenty seconds, then place in warm water for several hours.

Dried Arrangements

During winter months when fresh flowers were not available, dried flower arrangements were quite popular. These arrangements were often called everlastings. The two flowers most often mentioned in descriptions of the everlastings are amaranths and pearly everlastings.

The basic idea in drying flowers is to remove moisture as quickly as possible from the plants, without altering their appearance. There are three common methods for drying flowers, only two of which were available to Grandma. Air drying was the most common method among old-fashioned gardeners. The housewife dedicated to the art of dried flower arranging would sometimes use a dessicant, usually sand. Another favorite moisture remover was a combination of two parts borax to ten parts cornmeal. This had the disadvantage of being useful only once, but it was an inexpensive and effective means of drying blossoms. Today we have other easy-to-use dessicants, particularly silica gel. Modern gardeners can also use a microwave oven to dry herbs and flowers quickly, a luxury our grandmothers never dreamed of.

No matter what method you use, the plant material should be in the best possible shape. Any blemishes are magnified once a plant is dried. No matter how well plants dry, colors change slightly. Reds and purples turn dark or even blue; yellow and green fade; white turns cream or beige; and oranges sometimes turn red. Flowers picked past their prime usually turn brown. Air drying works well for plants that dry well naturally and retain their shape and color, such as grasses and seed heads, or flowers such as goldenrod, blue salvia, and larkspur.

Remove foliage and hang it upside down in small bunches in a dark, well-ventilated room. Grandma usually used a corner of the attic, but a shed or part of a garage will work as well.

Plants with large blossoms or those that retain a great deal of moisture, such as zinnias, daffodils, tulips, and marigolds, are best dried with a dessicant. Put a layer of silica gel (or sand for the authentic florist) in a tin cake pan or plastic storage box. Place the blossoms upside down, nestling them in the silica gel. Gently pour more gel over the blossoms until they are completely covered.

Once completely dry, flowers can be made into arrangements that should, with care, last several years.

The sense of completeness and livableness that is afforded by flowers about the house is a unique thing that can be achieved in no other way." *Garden magazine, (July 1924)*

Polyantha Rose

Wax Flowers

It has always been a challenge to see how long flowers can be preserved once they leave the garden and come into the home. During the mid-1800s waxing became quite popular as a preservation technique. With the introduction of paraffin, a by-product of the growing petroleum industry, housewives began experimenting with preserving floral beauty with this clear wax.

Wax flowers even made it into the flower shows. In 1927 Mrs. Malcolm Fleming of Atlanta sparked national interest with her waxed floral arrangement, a description of which appeared in the Garden Club of America *National Bulletin*: "under a glass capsule about eighteen inches high (was) . . . an old-fashioned bouquet of flowers—fresh from her garden but dipped in wax—in imitation of the Victorian wax ornaments of our grandmother's corner 'what-nots.' The glass cover was to protect the wax flowers from—well, perhaps we'd better not mention coal dust. It isn't patriotic."

Waxings succeeded only about half the time, but the successes made the failures more than worthwhile, even though wax dulls the naturally bright colors of blossoms. Not all flowers are suitable for waxing; those with hollow stems and flowers with heavy petals such as chrysanthemums, zinnias, and daylilies do not do well.

It is best to choose brightly colored blossoms that will look good when lightened by wax, white being best of all. Flowers that wax well are lilies of the valley, sweet peas, mock-orange blossoms, daisies, waterlilies, and fully opened roses. Foliage that waxes well includes holly, mahonia, privet, and pyracantha.

To wax fresh flowers, melt a large chunk of paraffin in an old saucepan. Because paraffin melts at a low temperature, it is possible to dip the flowers into the hot wax without ruining them. Carefully dip the entire blossom into the melted wax, shaking off any excess. Stand the flower in a bottle and allow the blossom to harden completely. This usually takes between ten and fifteen minutes. Once the blossom has thoroughly cooled, wax the stem by slowly spooning paraffin over stem and leaves. Again, set the flower in a bottle and allow it to harden for several hours.

Waxed flowers exposed to the air lose their color faster than those in an air-tight container. For this reason, ladies during Victorian times would often place their wax arrangements under glass domes to preserve them. It is also possible to wax dried flowers, a process that ensures the longevity of dried arrangements. Once the blossoms have been dried, use a paintbrush to cover the flowers with melted wax (130 degrees Fahrenheit). Allow to harden completely. Waxed dried flowers will be unaffected by the air and will retain their colors a very long time.

For an updated version of this craft, use liquid floor wax on evergreen leaves and berries to create a long-lasting holiday decoration.

The best leaves to use include holly, ivy, laurel, vinca, and euonymus. Berries that work well include hawthorn, holly, nandina, mahonia, bittersweet, and privet. Though they will eventually change colors, waxed leaves and berries retain their original colors for several months, making them ideal to use to decorate Christmas gifts.

Tussie-mussies and the Language of Flowers

Dried and fresh flowers can also be used to make nosegays and tussie-mussies. A tussie-mussie is a small bouquet arranged on a doily or piece of lace, tied with ribbons and presented to a lover or friend.

In Victorian England, each flower in the tussie-mussie had a particular meaning as defined by the language of flowers.

The language of flowers was introduced to England from Turkey. It evolved into a very intricate and complicated method of communication, with several dictionaries giving specific meanings for many different flowers. One of the most popular of these was Kate Greenaway's *Language of Flowers*, first published in 1884 and reprinted in 1978.

Even the way in which a flower was presented could be interpreted in different ways. For example, if a blossom were upright, it conveyed a happy, positive thought. The same flower presented upside down could mean the opposite. If the message referred to the sender, the flowers were tilted left; if the message referred to the recipient, right. Tussie-mussies became a very popular way to communicate with a loved one. They made a lovely, sweet-smelling gift, particularly if accompanied by a card explaining the meaning of each flower.

To make a tussie-mussie, cut an *x* in the center of a large lace doily. Choose a large, perfectly shaped blossom for the center, a rose perhaps, and stick the stem through the center of the doily. Fill in around this with bits of smaller flowers and foliage. A perfect tussie-mussie for the love of your life might include a red rose (love and desire), surrounded by small white carnations (pure and ardent love), a few pieces of fern (fascination), and a sprig of forget-me-not (true love and friendship.)

Wrap all stems with damp paper towels, cover them with plastic wrap or foil, and seal with green florist's tape. This should last for several days. To dry, submerge the entire tussie-mussie in silica gel and allow to dry thoroughly.

SAMPLER OF FLOWER AND HERB MEANINGS

alyssum, sweet: worth beyond beauty

amaranth, globe: immortality, unfading love

amaryllis: pride

aster: elegance and daintiness, talisman of love

bachelor's button: celibacy

begonia: beware! I am fanciful

bellflower (white): gratitude

bluebell: constancy, delicacy, and humility

carnation (pink): floral emblem of Mother's Day

carnation (purple): antipathy and capriciousness

carnation (red): admiration

carnation (striped): refusal

carnation (white): pure and ardent love, good-luck gift to woman

carnation (yellow): disdain

Christmas rose: relieve my anxiety

chrysanthemum (red): I love

chrysanthemum (white): truth

chrysanthemum (yellow): slighted love

clematis: mental beauty

cockscomb: affectation

columbine: cuckoldry and deserted lover, bad-luck gift to man

columbine (purple): resolved to win

columbine (red): anxious and trembling

coreopsis: always cheerful

crocus: abuse not

crocus, spring: youthful gladness

crocus, saffron: mirth

cyclamen: diffidence, bad-luck gift to woman

daffodil: regard

dahlia: instability

daisy: innocence, gentleness

daisy, garden: I share your sentiments

day lily: coquetry

fern: fascination

fern, maidenhair: discretion

flax: domestic industry

forget-me-not: true love, forget me not

foxglove: insincerity

frittilary, crown: majesty, power

fuschia: taste, amiability

geranium: folly and stupidity

geranium, scarlet: comforting

geranium, wild: piety

gladiolus: you pierce my heart

heliotrope: devotion

hibiscus: delicate beauty

hollyhock: ambition

honesty: honesty

hyacinth: sport, game, play

impatiens: refusal and severed ties

iris: faith, wisdom, and valor

iris, German: flame

jasmine (white): amiability

jasmine (yellow): timidity and modesty

larkspur: open heart and ardent attachment

lily (orange): hatred

lily (white): sincerity and majesty

lily of the valley: purity and jealousy

morning glory: farewell and departure

narcissus: egotism and conceit

nasturtium: conquest and victory in battle

pansy: thoughtful recollection

peony: healing

petunia: anger and resentment

phlox: sweet dreams and proposal of love

poppy: eternal sleep and oblivion

primrose: early youth and young love

rose (pink): our love is perfect happiness

rose (red): love and desire

rose (white): charm and innocence

rose (white and red): unity

rose (yellow): infidelity

rosebud: beauty and youth

rose, withered: fading beauty, reproach

Saint John's wort: superstition

sedum: lover's wreath

snapdragon: presumption and desperation

snowdrop: hope and consolation

sunflower: homage and devotion

sweet pea: departure and adieu

tiger lily: wealth and pride

tuberose: dangerous pleasures

tulip: symbol of the perfect lover

verbena: may you get your wish

violet: modesty and simplicity

wallflower: friendship in adversity

yarrow: disputes and quarrels

zinnia: thoughts of absent friends

Potpourri

Today the word *potpourri* is a term used casually to mean a mixture of different things, but originally it meant a blend of dried herbs, flowers, spices, and oils. The word is from the French *pourrir* and literally means "to rot." The first potpourri was a moist mixture of rose petals, pickled or preserved with salt and spices.

During American colonial days, potpourris were used throughout the house. China "potpourri jars" came in elaborate designs with beautiful decorations. They were created to allow either a little or a great deal of fragrance to be released into the air. Potpourri mixtures were also put into small sachet bags, which were tucked into drawers and cabinets to sweetly scent clothing, sheets, and blankets. Herb pillows were small pillows stuffed with potpourri. These were thought to induce sleep and assure one of pleasant dreams.

Moist potpourri has an advantage over a dry mixture in that the scent will last much longer. The disadvantage is that the mixture looks like a gooey mess and should be put into a container that cannot be seen through. The following recipe is from Maggie Oster's *Gifts and Crafts from the Garden*:

Moist Potpourri

1 quart rose petals
2 cups partially dried, fragrant flowers of your choice
1 cup partially dried, fragrant leaves, such as those of rose, geranium, lemon verbena, rosemary or lemon thyme

1 tablespoon powdered orris root
3/4 cup non-iodized salt
1/4 cup ground allspice
1/4 cup crushed cloves
1/4 cup brown sugar
2 crushed bay leaves
2 tablespoons brandy

1. Dry rose petals for three days.
2. Add partially dried, fragrant flowers and leaves.
3. Toss these ingredients with powdered orris root.
4. In a separate bowl, combine salt, spices, sugar, and bay leaves.
5. In a crock or wide-mouthed jar, alternate layers of the petals and herbs with the salt and spices. Sprinkle brandy over the top, and cap the crock or jar tightly, using a lid or plastic wrap. Stir daily with a wooden spoon.

The potpourri will be ready in about a month and should last for years.

Many recipes exist for making dry potpourri. All of them combine dried flower petals, leaves, herbs, essential oils, and fixatives. Fixatives slow down the evaporation of the fragrant oils found in plant materials. Although many different fixatives are used, perhaps the most common and most popular is orris root (*Iris X germanica* var. *florentina*). This violet-scented root has been used for centuries in the manufacture of potpourris. The only drawback to using the orris root is that some people have an allergic reaction to it. Use sparingly until you have determined your own reaction.

Other herbal fixatives include sweet flag, oak moss, ground and dried rosemary, sandalwood, and tonka beans. A general rule of thumb is to use one tablespoon of fixative per quart of dried flowers and herbs.

Essential oils are included to enhance the natural scent of the mixture. These can be of either the same scent as your dried flowers (such as rose oil with rose petals) or a complementary scent. No more than two tablespoons of essential oils should be added to the potpourri.

The following basic recipe can be adapted to your own needs and resources:

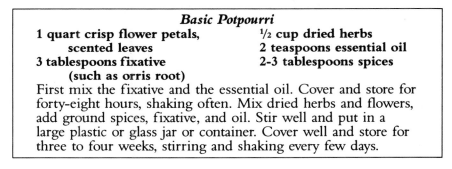

Basic Potpourri	
1 quart crisp flower petals, scented leaves	½ cup dried herbs
	2 teaspoons essential oil
3 tablespoons fixative (such as orris root)	2-3 tablespoons spices

First mix the fixative and the essential oil. Cover and store for forty-eight hours, shaking often. Mix dried herbs and flowers, add ground spices, fixative, and oil. Stir well and put in a large plastic or glass jar or container. Cover well and store for three to four weeks, stirring and shaking every few days.

Plant Material for Potpourri

Flowers

carnations	gardenia	sweet pea
chamomile	rose	tuberose
heliotrope	violet	wallflower
honeysuckle	lily of the valley	hyacinth
hyssop	mock orange	geranium
jasmine	stock	lavender
lilac		

Herbs and spices

rosemary	allspice	mint
pine needles	lemon verbena	nutmeg
southernwood	orange peel	vanilla
sweet woodruff	cinnamon	lemon balm
thyme	cloves	lemon thyme
basil	ginger	lemon peel

Selecting and harvesting plants for potpourri should be a twelve-month project. Search out violets in spring, roses in summer, and rosemary just before frost in fall. The best time of day to gather plant material is in late morning on a bright, sunny day. Flowers have their peak fragrance just after they have opened.

Harvest stems of plants, then gently pull the petals off. Spread these in a single layer on newspaper or, preferably, a piece of screen, to allow for better air circulation. Leaves can be hung upside down in bunches or stripped from the stem and spread on a piece of screen. Make sure that all plant material is thoroughly dry before making potpourri, or mold could easily develop, ruining the entire mixture.

Store plant material in glass or plastic air-tight containers in a dark place until you are ready to make the potpourri. Late fall is the perfect time to combine your flower harvest because potpourri and related crafts make wonderful Christmas presents. Potpourri can be used a variety of ways. The most common, of course, is in a potpourri jar while crushed potpourri is sometimes put into small cloth bags to make sachets to use in clothes drawers and linen closets. The sachets themselves can be as elaborate or as simple as you wish. Although cotton muslin is quite sufficient, delicately colored Victorian-patterned fabric will add a special touch to your gift. Tie with a satin ribbon or add a piece of lace or two, and your gift is sweet-smelling as well as visually appealing.

Sometimes potpourri was used to make herbal pillows or "sleep bags," as they were called in colonial America. These sleep bags were common gifts to the ill in the hope that the pillows would foster sleep and healing. The pillows were usually flat and designed to slip between regular pillows.

Cloth-covered wooden hangers filled with potpourri also make lovely gifts. Take a regular wooden hanger and measure from the hook to the end of the hanger. Cut two pieces of fabric, two inches wide and the length of the hanger. With right sides together, fold each piece of fabric in two, long sides together. Sew, using a quarter-inch seam along the end and the long side of the fabric. Turn so that the fabric is right-side-out. Repeat with the other piece. Slip the hanger ends into the fabric. Stuff lightly with polyester fiberfill and generously sprinkle potpourri into each side. Where the two fabric pieces meet at the hook, sew them together carefully.

Garden Dyes

Between 1750 and 1850, affectionately known as the "homespun" years on the American frontier, frontier settlers depended on the skills, resourcefulness, and stamina of housewives for most of their needs. Just as the family garden provided most of the food for the table, spinners and weavers in the family provided most of the clothing.

The threads and yarns that went into this clothing were rarely left their natural colors, however, because part of clothing's charm lies in the colors that can be created with dyes. In colonial America must of the dyeing was done in the larger cities and towns by skilled craftsman from Europe. But the housewife, far from the cities in terms of distance and money, relied on plants from the woods and her garden to transform her simple homespun into garments of color and richness.

Although elaborate recipes are available for dyeing yarn and cloth, really only a few basic principles must be followed. The cloth or fibers must be clean and free of chemicals and dirt. A mordant is necessary to help set the colors and keep them from bleeding during washing, and the plant material must be prepared and made into a dye bath.

WASHING OR CLEANING FIBERS: Use only 100 percent wool, cotton, or silk. Wool yarn is the easiest to dye. Use a mild soap to wash thoroughly the yarn or fabric to be dyed. Rinse thoroughly.

MORDANTS: Different mordants will create different colors from the same plant material. The following amounts are suitable for dyeing one pound of wool:

Aluminum — Potassium aluminum sulfate (also called alum) is the most stable and commonly used mordant. Produces bright shades and has good light fastness. Use four tablespoons plus four teaspoons cream of tartar.

Chrome — Potassium dichromate. This is unstable in light, so keep a cover over it. Warms color tones, enhances yellows and reds, mutes greens, softens wool. Use one tablespoon.

Tin — Stannous chloride brightens most colors but is hard on fibers and may make them brittle. Be sure to rinse fibers several times. Use two teaspoons.

Iron — Ferrous sulfate greys the yarn but gives good, dark colors. Called a saddener. Use two tablespoons.

Copper — Copper sulfate darkens colors and gives a greenish cast but good light fastness. Use two tablespoons.

THE DYE BATH: Rita Buchanan, author of *The Weaver's Garden*, suggests the following general procedures for creating a dye bath:

(1) Shred fresh, soft plant parts such as flowers and leaves into a pan, cover with water, and simmer for a half-hour to an hour, or until the water is colored and the tissues look bleached out. If the flowers or leaves have been dried, soak for several hours or overnight, then simmer in the same water.

(2) Press down on juicy fruits or berries to break the skins, then cover with water and add a little vinegar. Soak a few days at room temperature for best results, or heat to 150 degrees Fahrenheit for a half-hour.

(3) Chop or grind hard material such as roots, bark, or nut hulls into chips. The smaller the chips, the better the dye flows.

To premordant wool, put four gallons of water per pound of cleaned wool in a large dyepot. Add the recommended amount of mordant to a cup of boiling water. Add water with mordant to dyepot. Stir well. Wet wool thoroughly then carefully add to the dyepot. Simmer for an hour, remove the pot from the stove, and allow it to cool. At this point, the wool can be dyed immediately or stored. To dye, soak wool in water for a half-hour. Then place it in the dyebath and slowly bring to a boil. (Do not change temperatures quickly or drastically.) Leave it in the dyebath until the desired shade is obtained. Flower dyes usually take about a half-hour. Dyes from roots or bark may take one to two hours. Rinse the dyed wool several times, with cooler and cooler water, until the water is clear. Then gently squeeze out excess water and hang the wool in a shady spot to dry.

Not all plants, no matter how beautifully colored, are suitable for creating a dye. Experiment with plants from your own garden or use one of the following:

Dye from balm blossoms steeped in water produced a pretty rose color recommended for the linings of children's bonnets and for ribbons. *The American Frugal Housewife (1833)*

PLANT	COLOR	MORDANT
Black-eyed Susan (flowers)	green	chrome
Chamomile (flowers)	yellow	chrome or alum
Comfrey (leaves)	brown	iron
Dandelion (flower)	yellow	alum
Elderberry (berries)	violet	alum
(berries)	blue-grey	tin
(berries)	blue	chrome
(bark)	grey	iron
Goldenrod (flowers)	gold	chrome
Iris, purple (flowers)	blue/violet	chrome
Lily of the valley (leaves)	green	alum
Marigold (flowers)	yellow	chrome
Onion (red skins)	reddish-orange	alum
(yellow skins)	burnt orange	alum
(yellow skins)	brown	iron
Pokeweed (berries)	red	alum
(berries)	rust	chrome
Rosemary (leaves, flowers)	yellow-green	alum
Sage (tops)	green-grey	iron
Tansy (tops)	dark green	iron
Yarrow (leaves, flowers)	olive green	iron
Zinnia (flowers)	yellow	alum

ROSE PETAL BEADS

Few people will argue that roses are among the most sweetly scented of all flowers. To capture this essence and carry it with you, it is possible to make small beads from rose petals. Historically, these beads were used to create rosaries, carried by Catholic priests and nuns.

Rose beads are not difficult to make, but they do take an enormous amount of rose petals and quite a bit of time and patience. Start with about one-half bushel of fresh rose petals. Chop them up fine, macerate them using a mortar and pestle, or if you are firmly tied to the twentieth century, put them into a blender until you get a dull paste.

Put the paste into an iron saucepan or skillet and just barely cover it with water. Simmer for about an hour, let the paste cool, and simmer for another hour. The iron from the pan will react with the rose petals, making them a rich, dark color.

Every day for the next fourteen, work the paste with your hands or macerate with a mortar and pestle. Do this until the paste can be easily made into small beads. According to a nineteenth-century recipe, "When thoroughly well-worked and fairly well-dry, press on to a bodkin (a long hairpin) to make the holes in the centres of the

Plant a seed of a gourd and run for your life! — *Robert Sanders, Men's Garden Club of America*

beads. Until they are perfectly dry, the beads have to be moved frequently on the bodkin or they will be difficult to remove without breaking them."

If a bodkin is unavailable, a large embroidery needle will work nicely. However it is done, a hole must be pierced through the center of the beads, and the beads must be turned daily as they dry so that the hole is kept free. Drying time will last from ten to fourteen days, but once dry the beads will last for years and years and will emit a lovely rose fragrance every time they are worn.

GOURD CRAFTS

Gourds are rather bizarre-looking vegetables that are completely inedible, have no scent, and could never be considered really pretty. But they are so interesting and so odd-looking that gardeners have grown them for centuries.

Gourds come in a variety of shapes and colors. Many of their names reflect these characteristics: bottle, caveman's club, dolphin, Hercules's club, penguin, serpent, spoon, striped pear, Turk's turban, warty, and nest egg. Because of their hollow shapes and hard, outer shells, gourds have been used as containers, dipping utensils, even musical instruments. Gourd crafts have always been popular. The plants can be painted or carved and be used as Christmas tree ornaments, bird houses, bowls, wall hangings, or a host of other things.

Before you craft a gourd, it is important to condition and dry it properly. Harvest gourds before a frost and, because at first the outer skin will be soft, handle them very tenderly. Thoroughly clean your gourds with warm, soapy water, then rinse in a weak solution of disinfectant, such as Borax. Wipe them with a clean cloth and place on a layer of newspaper. Do not let the gourds touch one another and allow for good air circulation.

After they have been cured, the gourds should be wiped again with a disinfectant and can be waxed with a paste wax. For an especially shiny appearance, paint them with a clear varnish.

Gourds are wonderful to use in a variety of Christmas crafts. The tiny crooknecked ones can be painted in bright red and green to hang on the tree. Slightly larger ones can be cut and used as containers for a cheerful holiday arrangement.

To make a birdhouse, take a large, hard-shelled gourd, cut a hole one-and-one-quarter to one-and-one-half inches across toward the bottom and hang outside. To make a feeder, cut a larger hole and fill with bird seed.

The loofah gourd makes wonderful bath cloths and sponges. Grandma used them often for scrubbing dishes and furniture as well as herself in the bath, and in spite of the fact that synthetic sponges are cheap and readily available, natural loofah sponges remain quite popular.

70

BEAUTY FROM THE GARDEN

Herbs and flowers from the garden have supplied ladies with cosmetics, herbal baths, skin lotions, and hair and body ointments for centuries. Some of these beauty secrets are based on superstition, their worth being dependent upon the faith of the user. For example, raindrops collected in the base of the small wildflower Venus's looking glass were thought to make a woman attain beauty beyond belief. Dewdrops gathered on flowers before sunrise on May 1 were believed to get rid of freckles. Other beauty treatments contained ingredients that were dependably useful. The following recipes, though not guaranteed to take away wrinkles and restore youthful beauty, are often helpful in looking and feeling one's best.

Herbal Baths

Herbs can create a variety of effects in the bath. A true beauty bath in Grandma's day would have included dried lavender flowers, dried rosemary leaves, dried mint, chopped comfrey roots, and thyme made into an infusion and added to the bath. According to legend, however, this beauty bath will work only for those who think virtuous thoughts.

Herbs can be added directly to the bath water, but to make the clean-up a little easier, it is best if they are contained in a small cheesecloth bag. To make a bathtub-sized "tea" bag, place one-half cup of dried herbs in a square of cheesecloth and add to warm bath water.

Herbs can also be added in the form of soap bubbles, oils, or an infusion. To make an herbal infusion, pour two cups of boiling water over a half-cup of dried herbs, and allow to steep ten to twenty minutes. Remove the herbs and pour the infusion into the bath water. To create a bath oil, add three parts vegetable or nut oil to one part flower oil (such as rose or lavender). According to Rodale's *Encyclopedia of Herbs*, the best time to add the oil is after you have soaked in the tub for ten minutes or so. This allows the skin to absorb moisture from the water before the oil coats the skin.

To make scented bath bubbles, add one-eighth ounce flower oil to two cups Ivory Liquid. Allow the mix to stand about a week, then use a quarter-cup per bath.

Different herbs create different effects on the body. For a stimulating bath, use basil, bay, calendula flowers, horseradish roots, lemon verbena, mint, pine needles, rosemary, sage, or thyme. For a soothing bath, try catnip, chamomile flowers, elder, jasmine flowers, lemon balm, passionflowers, rose flowers, tansy flowers, or violets. For stiff and aching muscles, sage, strawberry leaves, chamomile, or comfrey is good. Blackberry leaves can provide a midwinter pick-me-up. An infusion of evening primrose flowers, mullein, or valerian roots creates a tension-relieving bath. To stimulate circulation, use equal parts of marigold and nettle. For softer skin, mix oatmeal and powdered milk with chamomile, calendula, and elder flowers.

To make scented soap balls, use an infusion from one of the following herbs: lavender flowers, mint leaves, rosemary, sage, or thyme. Add several drops of a complementary scented oil and steep ten to fifteen minutes. Grate two cups of Ivory soap, pour the infusion over the soap, and work with the hands until blended well. Make into small soap balls and place on plastic wrap to dry for thirty-six hours.

Facials and Hair Rinses

Steaming the face with various herbs is helpful for thorough cleansing. The easiest way to do this is to pour about one quart of boiling water over one-quarter cup dried herbs in a bowl. Lean over the bowl and make a tent with a towel to enclose your face. Let as little of the steam escape as possible.

As with baths, different herbs create different effects. For congestion, use eucalyptus, lavender, mint, or sage. Lavender, lemon balm, mint, rosemary, sage, or thyme makes a good energizer. To relieve tension, use catnip, chamomile, hops, jasmine, or linden. For a general cleansing facial use a combination of any of the following herbs: mint, elderberry flowers, comfrey, rosemary, yarrow, lemon balm, and lavender.

Herbs can also be used to make a hair rinse. The three herbs best known for hair care are rosemary, sage, and chamomile. Basil was often used to make the hair shiny. Rosemary and sage are used most often for brunettes; chamomile, for blondes.

TYPICAL SUMMER PLANTS FROM GRANDMA'S GARDEN

Common name: AJUGA
Botanical name: *Ajuga reptans* var. *alba*
Introduced: Brought to the U.S. between 1850 and 1900
Description: Ajuga is a rather stumpy-looking perennial ground cover most often grown for its foliage, which is evergreen in mild climates. The leaves are often reddish-brown, bronze, or variegated. During mid-summer short spikes of blue trumpet-shaped flowers develop. *A. reptans* has spikes of white flowers, which grow about ten inches tall.
How to grow: Ajuga should be grown in full sun or partial shade and does well in a wide variety of soil types. It is easily propagated by dividing and replanting clumps in spring or fall. For fast coverage of an area, space the plants six inches apart.
How to use: Ajuga is most useful as a ground cover.

Several common names are associated with ajuga. Bugleweed, common bugle, carpet bugle, middle comfrey, and sicklewort are all used to refer to this plant. Another name, carpenter's herb, refers to the superstition that this plant helped soothe thumbs inadvertently hit by careless carpenters.

There is some question as to the real medicinal value of ajuga. It does contain tannin, an astringent useful in stopping bleeding; therefore, the plant must have some healing value. It has been believed to cure such varied complaints as rheumatism, coughs, and liver disorders.

Common name: ALYSSUM
Botanical name: *Alyssum saxatile*
Introduced: Introduced to the U.S. between 1850 and 1900
Description: Alyssum is a low-growing perennial characterized by masses of small white or yellow flowers that come in early spring. A double form is now available, though the old-fashioned single is considered more beautiful. Each flower consists of four petals and measures one to three inches across. The silver-grey foliage is evergreen in mild regions.
How to grow: Alyssum is not particular about its environment. It does prefer slightly acidic, well-drained soil and full sun. It starts easily from seed and should begin to bloom approximately six weeks after seeding. For vigorous new growth, shear back after blooming.
How to use: This is a good plant to use in a hanging basket or a rock garden. Since it spreads easily, alyssum is also effective as an edging plant.

Great confusion exists over the botanical names for this plant. It is found listed in the genuses *Alyssum*, *Aurinia*, and *Lobularia*. *Alyssum maritima*, commonly found listed as *Lobularia maritima*, has a pleasing honey-sweet scent.

The name *alyssum* is from two Greek words, *a* meaning "without" and *lysson*, meaning "madness." Alyssum, also called madwort, was considered a powerful herb for combating mental disorders and hydrophobia. An old folk superstition suggests that carrying a piece of alyssum will prevent anyone's becoming angry with you.

Common name: BABY'S BREATH
Botanical name: *Gypsophilia paniculata*
Introduced: Introduced to the U.S. between 1850 and 1900
Description: Perennial baby's breath is a shrubby plant that grows to a height of thirty-six inches. During summer months it is covered with tiny white blossoms. The leaves are slender and pointed and measure two-and-one-half to four inches long. Individual blossoms are only one-sixteenth inch across but appear in such great numbers that this otherwise unexceptional plant is rendered beautiful and showy. Annual baby's breath (*G. elegans*) is similar to the perennial species but is shorter, reaching a height of only twelve to twenty inches.
How to grow: Baby's breath needs alkaline and well-drained soil. In areas where the soil stays soggy throughout the winter months, the roots will rot. Full sun and mulch during the winter help this plant retain its greatest beauty. It can be propagated by taking stem cuttings in spring.
How to use: This light, airy plant adds wonderful texture to the perennial border. It is used extensively as a cut flower, for it lasts a very long time. Dried, it lasts indefinitely.

The annual species was used more often in old-fashioned gardens. Favorite varieties were *G. elegans* (Alba grandiflora), a white-flowered variety, and *G. elegans* (delicate pink), a pink strain.

Baby's breath is beautiful both fresh and dried. To dry, tie bundles together and hang upside down in a dark, airy place. The flowers can also be dried by placing them in a small amount of water, where they will dry upright.

Common name: BLACK-EYED SUSAN VINE
Botanical name: *Thunbergia alata*
Introduced: Unknown
Description: Black-eyed Susan vine is a tender perennial that produces attractive yellow flowers with black or dark purple centers. The blossoms, only one-and-one-half inches long, are trumpet-shaped. The vine grows quickly. During the warm summer months it can reach a height of five to six feet. The dark green leaves are arrow-shaped.
How to grow: This vine comes easily from seeds, which should be started indoors six to eight weeks before the last frost date. Germination is slow, taking fifteen to twenty days. The plants should be spaced about six inches apart. Some sort of support will be necessary, either a trellis, a pole, or an arbor. The vine will bloom best in full sun with spent flowers removed.
How to use: Although black-eyed Susan vine is most often trained on some sort of support, such as an arbor or a trellis, the plant is also sometimes used in hanging baskets or as a ground cover.

There are over one hundred species in the *Thunbergia* genus, but the species *alata* is of the greatest horticulture value. Although the small blossoms resemble the true black-eyed Susan (*Rudbeckia hirta*), they are in a different genus altogether.

Common name: CALADIUM
Botanical name: *Caladium* x *bicolor*
Introduced: Introduced to the U.S. between 1850 and 1900
Description: Caladiums are grown for their spectacular foliage rather than their insignificant blossoms. The leaves of this tropical plant are large, heart-shaped, and come in variegated colors of green, red, and pink. The blossoms are borne on a spadix.
How to grow: Caladiums show their best colors when grown in a shady area. The tubers need to planted at a depth of two inches in rich, organic soil once the earth has warmed in spring. In all but the warmest areas, caladiums should be grown as annuals or as potted plants. Once the leaves begin to turn brown from fall frosts, dig up the tubers and store them in a cool (but not freezing) spot. During the growing season they need to be kept evenly moist.
How to use: Caladiums add soft, beautiful color to a shady garden. They are low-growing plants and are good to use under high-branched trees.

Caladium

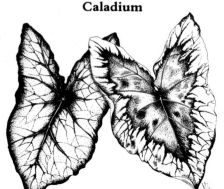

The outstanding foliage coloration of caladiums can be attributed to the French, who did great work in hybridizing this plant during the late 1800s. The Brazilians and Germans also did caladium breeding. In the United States the first work on this genus was done at the Missouri Botanical Gardens. All fifteen species in this genus are native to tropical areas.

Common name: CLEMATIS
Botanical name: *Clematis jackmanii*
Introduced: Hybrids (Gypsy Queen, Mrs. Cholmondeley) brought to the U.S. between 1850 and 1900
Description: Clematis is characterized by large star-shaped flowers. Each blossom is composed of eight petals surrounding a cluster of conspicuous stamen. Double varieties are available as well. Clematis is a vine ranging in length from one-and-one-half to five feet. Clematis blooms in spring and summer.
How to grow: This vine needs rich, fertile, well-drained soil and likes plenty of sunshine. The roots should be mulched heavily to protect them from drying out. Horticulturists say that it likes its head in the sun and its feet in the shade.

The British Jackman family, famous plant breeders, developed the hybrid *C. jackmanii* more than a century ago. Another old-fashioned cultivar is Nelly Moser, a pink-petalled variety with a dark pink midsection. The *Clematis* genus has over three hundred species, many native to eastern Asia and the Himalayas, while others are indigenous to England (*C. vitalba*) or the United States (*C. virginiana*). The English explorer and botanist Robert Fortune first brought clematis to England from China during the nineteenth century.

Clematis

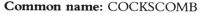

Common name: COCKSCOMB
Botanical name: *Celosia cristata*
Introduced: Brought to the colonies between 1700 and 1776
Description: Cockscomb is an annual characterized by large, brightly colored, exotic flower heads. There are two prevalent garden species. *C. agentea plumosa* has large, feathery plumes. *C.a. cristata* has a plume flattened into a fan shape and is often called a crested cockscomb. Flower colors include bright reds, pinks, gold, and apricot. The plants generally grow to be eighteen to twenty-four inches tall. Dwarf varieties are about twelve inches tall and spread nine to twelve inches.
How to grow: Cockscomb needs full sun or light shade and should be grown in rich, moist soil. It comes easily from seed, which can be sown directly into the garden once the soil has warmed in spring or can be started indoors six to eight weeks before the last frost date. Care should be taken not to transplant seedlings too deeply.
How to use: Cockscomb looks good planted in a mass or with other colorful annuals. Because of the intensity of its color, it is sometimes difficult to use it in a perennial border.

Cockscomb is generally useful to the flower arranger, for it is good as both a fresh cut flower and as a dried flower. To dry, hang bundles of cockscomb upside down in a dark, airy place and allow it to dry for several weeks.

In an 1835 issue of *Garden* magazine, Joe Breck gave specific instructions for growing cockscomb.: "Knight, in October 1820, sent to the Horticulture Society a cockscomb, the flower of which measured eighteen inches in width and seven inches in height, from the top of the stalk; it was thick and full, and of a most intense purple red. . . . The compost employed was of the most nutritive and stimulating kind, consisting of one part unfermented horse dung, fresh from the stable, one part burnt turf, one part of decayed leaves, and two parts green turf."

According to the Victorian language of flowers, cockscomb is considered a symbol for foppery, affectation, and singularity, apparently because of its ostentatious appearance. The genus name *Celosia* is from the Greek word *kelos*, meaning "burned," because of the bright orange and red colors of the blossoms.

Cockscomb

Common name: COLEUS
Botanical name: *C. blumei* var. *kirkpatrick*
Introduced: Introduced to the U.S. between 1850 and 1900
Description: The most outstanding characteristic of coleus is its colorful foliage. Patterned leaves display colors including green, chartreuse, white, gold, bronze, copper, red, pink, yellow, purple, and ivory. Leaf edges may be smooth or fringed, wavy or scalloped.
How to grow: Coleus needs at least partial shade but can be grown in deep shade as well, making it particularly appealing to those with limited sun. Nursery-grown plants are readily available, but the plant comes easily from seed as well. The seeds, which need light for germination, should be left uncovered when sowing. Plants should be spaced ten to twelve inches apart in rich, moist soil. Long spikes of small, inconspicuous flowers will form.

Although they can be left, removing them will prolong the bright foliage colors.

How to use: Coleus is useful in the shady garden. The bright foliage looks good with white blossoms or the grey shades of dusty miller or lamb's ears.

Over 150 species are found in the *Coleus* genus. The name is from the Greek word *koleos*, which means "sheath," and refers to the fact that the stamen are united into a sheath or tube. Leaves of some species are aromatic enough to have been used as flavoring.

Common name: CORNFLOWER
Botanical name: *Centaurea cyanus*
Introduced: Brought to the U.S. in 1600s
Description: Although newer varieties sport pink and even reddish colors, the original cornflower is a brilliant sky-blue. The plant has delicate green-grey foliage, and the entire plant stands about twenty-four to thirty-six inches tall. Dwarf varieties only twelve to fifteen inches tall are also available. Cornflower is an annual.
How to grow: Cornflowers need full sun and average garden soil. Seeds can be planted in fall or spring and should be sown one-quarter inch deep. Although the seedlings will need ample moisture to get established, after the first four to six weeks the plants are relatively drought tolerant.
How to use: Traditionally, cornflower has been included in informal gardens and naturalized plantings. The bright blue blossoms look wonderful coupled with many yellow or white garden flowers.

According to Katherine Whiteside's *Antique Flowers*, cornflowers were found among the treasures unearthed with King Tutankhamen's tomb. The name cornflower refers to the fact that this bright little wildflower grew profusely in fields of grain (called corn in England). An old superstition said that in bad years cornflowers, instead of grain, would grow from the seeds planted in fall.

Because cornflower has a stouter stalk than that of grain, many of the tools used to cut the grain would break when they hit the cornflower stalk. This led to the plant's common name, hurt sickle.

Cornflowers have been grown in England since 1629. There they were used as a medicine for inflamed eyes. The blossoms, boiled in beer, were also used to treat jaundice.

The genus name *Centaurea* is from the centaur Chiron, who was wounded by a nine-headed serpent and used blossoms from the cornflower to heal his wounds. The species name *cyanus* is from a mythical youth, Cyannus, who had a great love of flowers. After his death, Flora, goddess of the flowers, turned him into a cornflower. Another common name for the plant is bachelor's button, for the tight buds of the flower are so hard they were sometimes glued onto cloth as a replacement for buttons.

Common name: COSMOS
Botanical name: *Cosmos bipinnatus*
Introduced: Unknown
Description: Cosmos is a tall, delicate plant, growing to a height of twenty-four to thirty inches. The blossoms are white or pink; foliage is finely dissected and fern-like. Although double varieties are now available, most gardeners like the simplicity of the single blossom. *Cosmos sulphureus* is a smaller species native to the United States. These plants grow only twelve to eighteen inches tall and have bright orange or yellow blossoms.
How to grow: Cosmos can be easily grown from seed and blooms appear eight to ten weeks later. This plant does best in full sun or partial shade and thrives in well-drained, rich soil.
How to use: Cosmos can be used at the back of a border or in a naturalized, wildflower setting.

The name cosmos comes from the Greek word meaning "ordered universe" and was given to this flower because of the simple balance of the petals. Spanish priests are said to have grown these flowers in the monastery gardens. Giant Lady Lenox, a white, pink, and crimson variety, has been popular for many years. Klondyke, an old-fashioned variety, is smaller and yellow.

Common name: DAHLIA
Botanical name: *Dahlia juarezii*
Introduced: Introduced to the U.S. between 1800 and 1850
Description: Dahlias are best known for their vibrant color and variety of flower forms. Anemone forms have softly cupped and rounded petals; cactus forms have long, narrow, spinelike petals. Colors range from yellow and orange to red, white, cream, and pink.
How to grow: Dahlias are sun lovers and should be planted in rich, well-drained soil where they will receive at least six to eight hours of full sun daily. Dahlias, which require numerous nutrients, will benefit from frequent applications of fertilizers. The tubers are sensitive to the cold and must be dug up and stored before frost in early fall. In spring the tubers should be planted to a depth of six inches.
How to use: Because dahlias' foliage is often unkempt looking and the plants usually need staking, they are often planted in a cut flower garden rather than in an ornamental bed.

Double Dahlias

Dahlias were originally called cocoxochitl and were listed in a sixteenth-century Aztec herbal. When the Spanish first explored Mexico, they found this flower growing in the gardens there. Dahlias did not make it to Europe until the late eighteenth century when Spanish explorers in Mexico sent them to the king of Spain. By 1829 dahlias, considered the most fashionable flower in England, were used extensively in plantings in parks and other public places. By 1836 over one thousand varieties were available commercially to gardeners throughout Europe.

Common name: DAME'S ROCKET
Botanical name: *Hesperis matronalis*
Introduced: Brought to the U.S. in 1600s
Description: This plant stands approximately twenty-four to thirty-six inches high. The flowers, which occur in loose heads, are phlox-like and measure two inches across. They are white or light purple. The leaves are long and linear. The plant blooms in May and June.
How to grow: This perennial prefers full sun or partial shade and likes moist, well-drained soil. It grows quite easily from seed, which should be planted in spring after danger of frost has passed and the soil has warmed. It is a rather short-lived perennial and should be replanted every few years.
How to use: Dame's rocket is often included in wildflower meadow seed mixtures because it adapts so well to a field situation. Although it naturalizes well, it also looks good in more formal areas, if given sufficient room to grow and spread.

One of this plant's most oustanding characteristics is known only by those who venture into their gardens at night. The scent of this flower is practically indistinguishable during daylight hours, but as the sun sets the fragrance becomes stronger and stronger until the air is filled with its rich scent.

The botanical name refers to this trait, for *hesperis* is from the Greek word meaning "evening." *Matronalis*, of course, refers to a matron or dame.

Because of its outstanding fragrance, dame's rocket was at one time referred to as queen's gillyflower. Gillyflowers was a term used to refer to flowers, such as stock, carnations, and wallflowers, used in perfumes.

Although dame's rocket was popular with all women, it was a particular favorite of the French queen Marie Antoinette. Stories and legends tell us that during her imprisonment, she had bouquets of dame's rocket and pinks smuggled into her cell.

During the sixteenth century dame's rocket was used to induce sweating to break a fever. It was also used for treating wounds and curing scurvy.

Dame's rocket, often called sweet rocket, was included in many old-fashioned gardens. In the early 1800s one gardener wrote, "No garden ought to be without them; their neat habit, beauty, and particular fragrance alike recommend them."

Common name: DELPHINIUM
Botanical name: *Delphinium belladonna*
Introduced: *Delphinium ajacis* (larkspur) introduced before the eighteenth century; *Delphinium grandiflorum* (bouquet larkspur) brought to the U.S. between 1850 and 1900
Description: Delphinium is a tall, stately flower with spikes of blue to purple or sometimes white or pinkish blossoms. The foliage is dark green and deeply dissected. *D. belladonna* grows thirty inches tall and has white or dark blue blossoms. The flower's center, called the "bee," is sometimes a contrasting color.
How to grow: Delphiniums need cool summers and will not tolerate hot, humid conditions. The plants require rich, well-drained soil that is slightly

acidic to alkaline. Because of the abundance of blossoms and their height, delphiniums will generally need staking and protection from the wind. Plants should be divided in the fall or early spring, and divisions should be set out twenty-four inches apart.

How to use: Tall, beautiful delphiniums create a rich background for a perennial border. They show to their best advantage when planted against a wall or light evergreen hedge so that the dark blue blossoms do not get lost in the shadows.

In spite of its heavy, sultry beauty, the delphinium is considered a symbol of swiftness and lightness according to the Victorian language of flowers. The name delphinium is from the Greek word for dolphin, for to many people the seed pod of this plant resembled a dolphin. This same seed pod gave rise to other common names, such as larkspur, lark's heel, or lark's claw.

Ancient uses of delphinium include curing toothache, getting rid of lice, driving away scorpions, and fending off savage beasts. The species *D. consolida* was used to heal cuts or dress wounds; the species name is from the Latin word meaning "to close together." Delphinium is extremely poisonous and should never be taken internally.

Probably the oldest garden delphinium is *D. staphisagria*, native to the Mediterranean region. Probably grown in gardens since at least the fifteenth century, it was usually cultivated for its power to drive away bugs rather than for its beauty. By 1890 many varieties were available in both single and double forms. Belladonna delphiniums were used for cut flowers, and *D. ranunculoides* was often planted in the ornamental garden because its sterile flowers last longer than fertile blooms.

Only relatively recently were new colors of delphiniums introduced. Yellow, cream, and white were not available until 1895; pink, until 1960.

Common name: FLOWERING TOBACCO
Botanical name: *Nicotiana alata* var. *grandiflora*
Introduced: Introduced to the U.S. between 1850 and 1900
Description: Flowering tobacco is a summer annual with large (two- to two-and-one-half-inch) trumpet-shaped blossoms of white, crimson, pink, lime green, or purple. The plant, covered with fuzzy, sticky foliage, grows to a height of twelve to fourteen inches. The blossoms are particularly fragrant during the early evening just as the flowers begin to open.
How to grow: Flowering tobacco likes full sun or partial shade and can tolerate hot summer conditions as long as the plants are well watered. It prefers rich soil and benefits from weekly applications of a liquid manure. If the dead flower heads are removed, the plant will continue to put forth blossoms throughout the summer. Seeds can be started indoors six to eight weeks before the last frost date or can be sowed outdoors after the soil has warmed. The seeds need light to germinate and should be left uncovered after sowing.
How to use: *Nicotiana* adds unusual texture and color to a mixed border. The fragrant blossoms are an extra bonus.

In 1915 J. Rutherford McFarland wrote of *Nicotiana* in his book *My Growing Garden*: "In the half-hour following the summer sunset, if the evening is still, there pervades in the garden the fragrance of this better tobacco, and its white flowers that open only when the sun has declined are as the garments of a fairy. On summer moonlight nights this Lady Nicotine is queen of the fairies, indeed."

Flowering tobacco was first found growing in the wilds of Brazil. It is a close relative of the commercial tobacco plant but does not hold the economic importance that its cousin does. The genus *Nicotiana* was named for Jean Nicot, a French consul to Portugal, who introduced tobacco to the courts of Portugal and France.

Flowering Tobacco

Common name: FOUR O'CLOCK
Botanical name: *Mirabilis jalapa*
Introduced: Brought to the colonies during the 1700s
Description: Four o'clocks have large, brightly colored, trumpet-shaped flowers that open late in the afternoon and stay open until the next morning. Flower colors include white, lavender, pink, yellow, and salmon. The plants grow to a height of forty-eight inches, and the blossoms measure twelve to twenty-four inches across.
How to grow: The plants are drought tolerant and can withstand relatively harsh conditions. They need full sun and cannot take soggy, poorly drained soil. Tubers may be dug in late fall and stored during the winter to be planted again in spring.
How to use: Because of their dense growth habit, four o'clocks can be used as an annual hedge. The plants grow very quickly and produce an enormous root system.

Four o'clock

The French call this plant *belle de nuit*; the Italians, *bella di notte*. Four o'clocks are members of the *Nyctaginaceae*, or "night blooming," family. Seeds were used by the Japanese for making cosmetics. The Chinese extracted a pigment from the blossoms to color gelatin made from seaweed.

Four o'clocks are also known as marvel of Peru. The genus name was at one time *Admiralis*, but Carolus Linnaeus changed it to *Mirabilis*, or "admirable."

Common name: FOXGLOVE
Botanical name: *Digitalis purpurea*
Introduced: Brought to the U.S. in 1600s
Description: The first year of growth of the biennial foxglove produces a large rosette of long-stemmed leaves. In the second growing season a tall spire of white or pink cup-shaped flowers appears. Inside each blossom are small reddish brown dots. The blossoms open progressively up the stem, creating a pyramid effect. Foxglove grows to a height of three to four feet.
How to grow: Foxglove grows best in rich, well-drained soil in full sun. In extremely warm areas it benefits from a bit of shade during the hottest part of the day. Nursery-grown plants can be set out during fall or spring and should be planted at least one foot apart. Seeds can be sown in late summer for bloom the following year. Do not cover seeds as they need light for germination.
How to use: Foxgloves create a good vertical backdrop for smaller perennials in the border. The tall, colorful spires add nice color to the early summer garden.

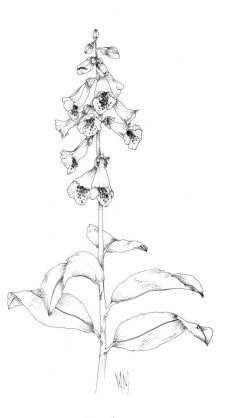

Foxglove

In 1760 John Bartram listed seeds of the yellow foxglove as part of a shipment of plants from England, the first official mention of foxglove in the United States although the plant was probably brought here years before that by English and German settlers.

The greatest contribution of foxglove was not its beauty as an ornamental garden plant, but its value as a medicinal herb. According to Clair Shaver Haughton's *Green Immigrants*, Dr. Hall Jackson of Portsmouth, New Hampshire, wrote in 1787 that he had just received a shipment of foxglove seed from a Dr. Withering in England. Dr. Withering asked him to "share the seed with interested men in other states who would cultivate it and spread the knowledge of this beneficent plant and its medicinal use."

Dr. Withering had cause to praise this plant because two years earlier it had brought him great honor and fame. Foxglove had long been thought of use in treating "dropsy," or heart problems. In 1775 Dr. Withering, a physician living in Shropshire, England, noticed that herb women in the area who used foxglove often had great success treating people suffering from heart problems. After much experimenting, Dr. Withering discovered the correct amounts needed to help his patients afflicted with heart disease.

Even today digitalin, a chemical found in the leaves of foxglove, is collected from the plant to create drugs used to combat heart disease. Interestingly, this chemical is impossible to duplicate synthetically, so the plant itself is necessary for the production of the drug.

Superstition still goes hand-in-hand with modern medicine, though, and folk healers will tell you that foxglove has medicinal purposes only if collected with the left hand.

If taken in incorrect amounts, toxic chemicals within foxglove can be deadly poisonous. This is not a plant to be used by the home herb healer.

Common name: FREESIA
Botanical name: *Freesia* (hybrids)
Introduced: Unknown
Description: Freesias are fans of small trumpet-shaped flowers. Blossom colors include yellow, orange, pink, red, purple, and violet. The leaves, which look like miniature gladiolus leaves, are broad and sword-shaped. Plants generally reach a height of one-and-one-half to two feet.
How to grow: Freesias, which grow from a slender corm, must be grown where temperatures do not dip below twenty degrees Fahrenheit, ideally where the summers are dry and the winters cool and moist. The plants are most often grown in a greenhouse or sunny window. Plant freesia in the fall at a depth of two to three inches, six to eight to a six-inch pot. They do best when exposed to night temperatures between forty-five to fifty-five degrees Fahrenheit. They will need watering as they grow.
How to use: Freesia is usually started indoors or in the greenhouse and then moved to the porch or window box during spring and summer months.

Although freesia blossoms are lovely, it was their heady sweet fragrance that endeared this plant to gardening ladies of the past. The flowers are effective in arrangements, lasting several days without showing any signs of wilting. Freesias are originally from South Africa. The two most common species are *F. refracta*, with greenish yellow flowers with brown markings, or *F. alba*, white flowers marked with yellow.

Common name: GAS PLANT
Botanical name: *Dictamnus albus* var. *rubra*
Introduced: Introduced to the U.S. between 1776 and 1850
Description: Gas plant is a rather shrubby perennial growing to a height of two to three feet. During late spring and early summer, spires of white or pink blossoms appear. Evergreen leaves are shiny and distinctly lemon-scented.

How to grow: Gas plants should be set out approximately three feet apart. They need full sun and well-drained soil rich in organic matter. Propagated from seed, it takes about three to four years to get a blooming plant. Once established, the plants should not be moved as they do not transplant easily.

How to use: Gas plant makes a good "background" plant, setting the stage for smaller, showier plants.

The common name gas plant derives from an unusual characteristic. During hot summer days, the flowers emit a volatile oil which, if lighted with a match, will burst into flames. For this reason it is also called burning bush. The genus was named for Mount Dicte in Crete.

Common name: GLADIOLUS
Botanical name: *Gladiolus gandavensis*
Introduced: Introduced to this country before the eighteenth century
Description: Long, sword-shaped leaves surround tall stalks of brilliantly colored flowers. Each flower stalk can stand as high as sixty inches and blooms in almost every color, including white and green.
How to grow: Corms should be started in successive plantings in spring and early summer. The corms should be planted to three times their depth; the larger the corm, the larger the blooms produced. Glads need bright, direct sunlight and rich, fertile soil.
How to use: Glads are used as a garden accent and as cut flowers. The blossoms last only a week, so they have limited use.

Gladiolus

Around the turn of the century, a contributor wrote in *Horticulture* magazine, "I fear *Gladiolus cardinalis* is hardly yet to be met with in the seed stores in Boston, but I trust it will soon become as much cultivated as its beauty deserves. In the meantime it may easily be procured from Holland or England where it is not a dear root." Every self-respecting garden in the late 1800s had a staff of glads in the summer garden despite the plant's relative dearness. Luckily for gardeners today, gladiolus is dear only in the sense that the flower is endearing, not that it is difficult to find in garden stores.

Glads make an extremely popular cut flower. Sheila MacQueen, the grande dame of English floral arranging, suggests picking the stalks when the buds are just beginning to show color. They can be left at this stage for a long time then put into warm water for the buds to open fully overnight.

Gladioli are thought to be the "lily of the field" that Jesus referred to in His Sermon on the Mount. They are sometimes referred to as "sword lilies" because of the leaf's shape. The genus name is from the Latin word meaning "sword."

The corms were beaten into a poultice used to draw out splinters or thorns and also mixed with goat's milk and used to treat colic.

According to the English floral calendar, glads are the flower for August.

Common name: GLOBE AMARANTH
Botanical name: *Gomphrena globosa*
Introduced: Brought to colonial gardens during the 1700s
Description: Globe flower, or globe amaranth, has clover-like, papery flower heads ranging in color from purple to lavender to white, pink, orange, and yellow. These annual plants grow to be thirty inches tall.
How to grow: Globe flower should be planted in spring after all danger of frost is past, using either nursery-grown plants or seedlings started indoors six to eight weeks earlier. If sowing seeds, allow them to soak in water three to four days before planting. Globe flower needs full sun and prefers light, well-drained, airy soil. This drought-tolerant plant easily withstands hot, dry conditions.
How to use: Because its individual flower heads are small, globe flower looks best when planted in a mass. It is good as a cut flower and makes an outstanding dried flower as well.

The flower's shape caused the genus name *Gomphrena*, for it comes from the Greek word *gomphos*, meaning "club." The common name amaranth is often used with this plant although the true amaranth is a different plant altogether. The name is useful descriptively, though, for it means "unfading" and alludes to the everlasting quality of the dried flowers.

Common name: HELIOTROPE
Botanical name: *Heliotropium arborescens*
Introduced: Brought to this country between 1776 and 1850
Description: Although heliotrope can grow to be six feet tall, the plant usually grows only twenty-four to thirty inches high. Flowers are borne in small clusters and are either white, blue, or purple. The leaves are deeply veined, thick, and crinkly.
How to grow: This plant is quite susceptible to the cold and should not be planted until all danger of frost is passed. If started indoors, the seeds should be sown ten to twelve weeks before planting time. Germination will take twenty to twenty-five days. Heliotrope does well in average garden soil, kept evenly moist and fertilized only once or twice. Heliotrope needs full sun. Plants should be spaced twelve inches apart.
How to use: Heliotrope is especially loved for its sweet fragrance and is often grown in containers, hanging baskets, or window boxes.

The genus name *Heliotropium* is from two Greek words meaning "turning toward the sun." The plant, however, does not follow the course of the sun. The species name *arborescens* means "shrubby."

Heliotrope was considered a symbol of love and admiration. According to Kate Greenaway's *Language of Flowers*, heliotrope is an emblem of devotion and faithfulness. Favorite old-fashioned varieties include Lemoines Giant and Elsie.

Heliotrope was introduced from Peru to England in 1757 by way of France. French botanist, Joseph de Jussieu, its original discoverer, was said to be "intoxicated with delight" by the plant. According to Leyel's book *Compassionate Herbs*, written in 1948, heliotrope was used to make a tincture of "great service in the clergyman's sore throat."

Heliotrope has a very sweet, fruity fragrance, which has given rise to names such as cherry pie. Two important Victorian varieties were Miss Nightingale and Beauty of the Boudoir.

David Stuart and James Sutherland, in their book *Plants from the Past*, say that heliotrope was essential to every high Victorian garden, grown outdoors during the summer and in the conservatory during winter months.

Common name: HOLLYHOCK
Botanical name: *Althaea rosea*
Introduced: Grown in American gardens since the 1600s
Description: Large hollyhock blossoms appear on tall spires, measure four to five inches across and bloom in yellow, red, purple, pink, and white. The plants can grow to a height of seventy-two to ninety-six inches. Older varieties are considered short-lived perennials or biennials. Newer strains can be grown as annuals.
How to grow: Hollyhocks need rich, well-drained soil and full sun. The old-fashioned varieties will invariably need staking because of their height.
How to use: Hollyhocks are good to use at the back of a border or along a fence line because of their height.

In 1631 hollyhocks were brought to the United States, where they gained instant popularity. By the early eighteenth century, double hollyhocks were quite popular here. In Europe hollyhocks were found in shades of pink and red. By the mid-nineteenth century hollyhocks were widely used at the back of borders. Dahlias were grown in front to hide the plant's "ugly shins."

Many of the strains grown in earlier centuries are no longer available, due in part to problems with rust disease that hit the flower hard in the late nineteenth century. Two of the ancient varieties that still exist include the marshmallow, *A. officinalis*, which was used extensively during the eighteenth century, and *A. cannabina*, a species loved by the English gardener and writer John Parkinson. One of the more popular old-fashioned varieties is Newport pink.

Hollyhocks are in the same family as cotton. Their juice, which is mucilaginous, was often included in children's cough syrups, for it seemed to have a soothing effect. The genus name means "that which heals" and was given for the plant's medicinal value. The name hollyhock comes from its profusion in the holy land, the original name coming from the Anglo-Saxon word *halig*, meaning "holy."

Both the blossoms and the small seed pods are edible and even considered quite tasty. According to the Victorian language of flowers, hollyhock means fruitfulness, presumably because of the abundance of flowers on a plant.

"Consider the hollyhock; how it grows! It seems both to toil and to spin, and then in result to be clothed in a gorgeousness to which the Solomon's glory would be mere manufacture," wrote J. Horace McFarland in his elegant book *My Growing Garden*.

Common name: HOSTA
Botanical name: *Hosta plantaginea*
Introduced: Introduced to this country between 1850 and 1900
Description: Large, variegated leaves are the most outstanding characteristic of this plant. The blossoms are also attractive and generally grow to be twenty-four to thirty-six inches tall and produce gently colored flowers. Much hybridization has been done to create a myriad of colors and leaf variations.
How to grow: Hostas perform best in shady areas when planted in rich, moist soil. Although they will tolerate full sun if given sufficient moisture, leaf variegation will be more distinct if the plant grows in shade. Plants can be divided in spring and replanted twelve to twenty-four inches apart depending on the size of species used.
How to use: Because of their oustanding foliage, hostas are great to use in a shady garden. Variation in leaf coloration makes for great interest within a hosta collection.

The old-fashioned name for hostas is funkia. Another common name is plantain lily. The genus was named for Nicholas Host, an early nineteenth-century plantsman who also served as doctor to the emperor of Austria. Hostas were introduced to English gardeners in 1780 but did not gain real popularity until relatively recently.

Common name: JACOB'S LADDER
Botanical name: *Polemonium caeruleum*
Introduced: Brought to the U.S. between 1776 and 1850
Description: Old-fashioned Jacob's ladder boasts medium blue flowers on a stalk bearing neat pairs of leaves, giving the entire plant the appearance of a small ladder. It grows to a height of eight to thirty-six inches and spreads twelve to twenty-four inches across. A white cultivar is also available. Jacob's ladder blooms from late spring into summer.
How to grow: This perennial prefers rich, loamy, well-drained soil and full sun. Hot sunshine might make the leaves turn yellow in midsummer if there is insufficient rainfall. Plants may be divided or sown from seed in spring.
How to use: Low-growing varieties are particularly good for the rock garden. The taller varieties are light and airy, providing nice texture and pleasant color to the perennial border.

The genus name *Polemonium* has two possible origins. The name may have derived from the Greek word for war. Pliny, a Greek writer, suggested that there was a brief "war" over who actually discovered this flower. The other possibility is that the flower was named for Polemon, a Greek philosopher living in Athens. The common name, of course, refers to the ladder-like configuration of the leaves, which someone thought to resemble the ladders to heaven that Jacob saw in his dream. Other common names for this plant include Greek valerian, charity, blue jacket, and poverty.

Jacob's ladder has been grown in English gardens since the time of the Roman occupation. It is indigenous to northern Great Britain and grows naturally as far north as Lapland.

Common name: LILY
Botanical name: *Lilium* sp.
Introduced: *Lilium canadense* (meadow lily) grown in American gardens during the 1600s
Description: There are between eighty and ninety known species of lilies, many of them native to the United States. In addition, plant breeders have developed many cultivars. Although there is tremendous variation within the genus, there are certain common characteristics. All lilies have six petal-like segments called tepals, usually curved backward at the tips. Six stamen are found within the blossom, and the inner tepals are often spotted. Blossoms may point either up or down.

How to grow: Lilies need rich, thoroughly tilled, and well-drained soil. If water stands on the bulbs, they will rot. Lilies can be planted in full sun or light shade. Ideally, the bulbs should be kept cool. This can be accomplished by overplanting with annuals or low-growing perennials or by using a deep layer of mulch. Lilies show tremendous variation in height. Anything over three feet should be staked. Bulbs should be planted in fall anywhere from four to eight inches deep.

How to use: Small native lilies can be used effectively in a woodland garden. Taller hybrids look spectacular in a more formal garden setting.

Lilies have been found in gardens for thousands of years. They were probably first cultivated in the Tigris-Euphrates Valley about five thousand years ago. The lily was considered a sacred flower of Venus, the Roman goddess of love and beauty. Lilies were also associated with Juno and were sometimes referred to as *Rosa junonis*, or Juno's rose.

During the nineteenth century the lily was considered a symbol of purity and innocence. Lilies are, according to the Victorian language of flowers, a symbol of majesty. In Victorian times lilies were popular in church decorations, but the stamen were always removed before the flowers were brought into the church so as not to offend anyone.

In Korea the tiger lily grows wild in profusion. It is appreciated for its beauty as well as for its delicate taste. Even today lily buds are considered a culinary delight. They are easily used by dropping them into a clear soup during the last few minutes of cooking.

In many European communities, lilies were thought to ward off witchcraft and ghosts.

Lilies to include in recreating an eighteenth-century garden are *L. superbum* and *L. philadelphicum*. Nineteenth-century lilies include *L. tigrinum*, *L. speciosum*, *L. auratum*, and *L. pardalinum*.

Common name: LOVE-IN-A-MIST
Botanical name: *Nigella damascena*
Introduced: Introduced to this country before the eighteenth century
Description: Love-in-a-mist displays delicate, thread-like foliage with blossoms of white, blue, purple, or pink. Each flower measures one-and-one-half inches across, with the plant reaching a height of twelve to twenty-four inches.

How to grow: Love-in-a-mist is an annual with a short blooming period. For best results, sow seeds in successive stages throughout spring and early summer so that continuous bloom is possible. Although the plant needs good drainage, it will thrive in average garden soil. It does require full sun. This plant does not transplant well and must therefore be sown in a permanent location. Seed germination takes approximately ten to fifteen days.

How to use: Love-in-a-mist blossoms are good as a cut flower, and the seed pods are useful in dried arrangements. The delicate foliage lends nice texture to the summer garden.

The genus name *Nigella* is from Latin and translates as the common name, love-in-a-mist, presumably a reference to its fine, mist-like foliage. This is an ancient plant and was most likely brought to England from

Damascus in 1570, thus the species name *damascena*.

Double varieties of the plant have been cultivated since 1597. One of the most popular old-fashioned varieties is Miss Jekyll, named for the eminent gardener Gertrude Jekyll. Other common names for the plant include gith (an Anglo-Saxon word for cornfield weed), St. Katharine's flower, fennel flower, devil-in-the-bush, love-in-a-puzzle, and love-entangle.

The species *N. sativa*, called nutmeg flower, was brought to England in 1548. It was cultivated for its aromatic seeds that were used as spice. Egyptians have sprinkled the seeds on bread and cakes since the time of the Pharoahs.

Common name: MARIGOLDS
Botanical name: *Tagetes erecta*
Introduced: French marigold grown in seventeenth-century colonial gardens
Description: There is tremendous variation among these annuals of the daisy family. Different varieties may be as short as six inches and as tall as thirty-six. Flower sizes range from three-quarters of an inch to five inches across, with colors ranging from white, yellow, and orange to cream. *T. erecta* is a tall African marigold with large flowers. *T. patula* is the French marigold, usually with double flowers in yellow and orange. *T. tennuifolia* has single flowers and grows only eight inches tall.
How to grow: Marigolds like full sun but can otherwise adapt to a wide range of environmental conditions. They prefer rich, well-drained soil but will grow and bloom in less fertile soil as well. Marigolds are easily grown from seed.
How to use: Because of the variations in size and color, marigolds fit into almost any part of a sunny garden. Small varieties can be used as edging, with the larger flowers taking a more prominent place in the flower bed. Tall varieties need to be staked.

Marigolds were first found growing in Brazil nearly four hundred years ago. The bright yellow flowers were held sacred by the Aztecs, who used them extensively in decorating temples and shrines on holy days. After the Spanish massacre, the Indians adopted the marigold as their emblem, with the red-streaked blossoms representing blood spilled by the Spaniards. For this reason they sometimes called the plant *flor de muerto*, the "flower of death."

Many country folks use marigolds in the vegetable garden to keep away pests. When released into the soil, chemicals within the root kill nematodes. Marigold was also used to heal wounds and get rid of warts.

The name marigold — "Mary's gold" — honors the Virgin Mary. Although the marigold was considered a sign of good luck, according to the Victorian language of flowers, marigold also means jealousy.

Common name: MIGNONETTE
Botanical name: *Reseda odorata*
Introduced: Brought to the U.S. between 1776 and 1850
Description: The stems of this thick, common-looking plant grow twelve to eighteen inches tall and bear spikes of small yellowish green blossoms. It is the wonderful scent of this plant that secures its spot in the garden year after year.

How to grow: Seeds of this annual should be planted in the garden after danger of frost has passed. The seeds need light to germinate, so they should be left uncovered. Germination will take five to ten days. Mignonette performs well in full sun or light shade and needs fertile, well-drained soil.
How to use: Because its fragrance is greater than its beauty, mignonette is often grown in containers, which are then arranged on a patio or deck to take best advantage of the scent.

"Success and good fortune will attend the lover who rolls three times in a bed of mignonette" goes the superstition. The sweet scent certainly could not hurt in the pursuit of love.

This plant is native to Egypt and was placed in tombs where the mummies were laid. The seeds were imported to Europe during the classical period. Mignonette had value as a medicine, primarily as a gentle sedative. The genus name is from the Latin and means "to calm."

The scent has been described as "highly ambrosial." Henry Phillips, an English gardener, wrote that mignonette was grown in London window boxes "until whole streets were almost oppressive with the odour." This plant was extremely popular during the early nineteenth century. Napoleon was said to have sent the seeds to his Empress Josephine for her garden at Malmaison.

Common name: MORNING GLORY
Botanical name: *Ipomoea purpurea*
Introduced: Brought to the U.S. between 1776 and 1850
Description: The original old-fashioned morning glory had a single, trumpet-shaped blue flower and large, heart-shaped leaves. Today many different colors are available, including pink, purple, and white. Double flower forms are also now available. These blossoms occur on slender vines that can grow as much as ten feet in a single growing season. The blossoms open first thing in the morning and usually fade by noon. A related species, *I. alba*, is called moonvine and has large, fragrant white blossoms that open in evening.
How to grow: Both moonvine and morning glory need full sun and a sandy, rich soil. Seeds should be started indoors four to six weeks before planting time in spring. If soaked overnight or nicked with a file, the seeds will germinate more quickly. Plant seeds in individual peat pots and transplant carefully.
How to use: On a trellis or fence near the kitchen window, morning glories make quite a treat for breakfast viewing.

Morning glories were imported from Mexico to Spain, where they gained great popularity. Because of their graceful growing habits, monks often used morning glory designs on the borders of manuscripts. Witches used morning glory in casting spells. The plant was thought to be particularly potent if used three days before a full moon.

Common name: NASTURTIUM
Botanical name: *Tropaeolum majus*
Introduced: Grown in colonial gardens during the 1700s
Description: Brightly colored five-petaled blossoms grow on low, trailing stems. Blossom colors include red, orange, and yellow. The leaves are almost perfectly round. Some species in this genus are almost bushy, growing only twelve inches high while others are vining and can grow eight feet or more.
How to grow: Nasturtiums need full sun and grow well in average, well-drained garden soil. The seedlings are particularly sensitive to cold, so the plants should not be sown in the garden until all danger of frost has passed.

How to use: Nasturtiums are lovely in the garden and tasty in the kitchen. The nutritious leaves are often used in salads.

The tart taste of the leaves gave rise to the common name for this plant. Nasturtium is from the Latin words meaning "nose twister." In days when scurvy was a problem on sailing ships, sailors took barrels of pickled nasturtium seeds with them on long voyages. Superstition suggests that eating nasturtium blossoms keeps muscles from getting stiff.

Common name: ORIENTAL POPPY
Botanical name: *Papaver orientale*
Introduced: French double poppies (red, scarlet, white, or blush) brought to the U.S. in the 1600s
Description: Oriental poppies have huge, showy blooms and are often black in the center. Blossoms are sometimes as much as twelve inches across, with the plant growing to a height of twenty-four to forty-eight inches. Blossoms come in a variety of colors including white, pink, and bright red. Corn poppy (*P. rhoeas*) is generally grown as an annual. It reaches a height of twenty-four to sixty inches and comes in an array of colors including red, orange, and pink. Iceland poppy (*P. nudicaule*) is considered a tender perennial. Blossoms measure three inches across and are red, orange, pink, yellow, cream, or white.
How to grow: Poppies perform best in cool weather in alkaline soil. The soil needs to be well drained and of average fertility. Poppies like plenty of moisture and should be positioned in full sun. Sow seeds in late spring for late summer blooms. Tall varieties should be staked.
How to use: Use in the border close to plants that can cover up the bare spots once the plant has bloomed and died back.

In ancient times poppies were associated with death and burial rituals. Egyptians felt that poppies were essential for assuring life after death, and dried petals have been found in Egyptian tombs dating back three thousand years.

Greeks used poppy seeds as a love charm and thought that they would bring strength and health. A tea made from the dried petals was used to soothe children with colic and whooping cough. During Elizabethan times, poppy syrup was used to relieve pain and induce sleep. English gardeners have grown and loved poppies for centuries. The English floral calendar considers poppies the flower for August.

Mrs. Perry and Mary Studholme are both salmon pink varieties quite popular at the turn of the century.

Common name: PETUNIA
Botanical name: *Petunia* x *hybrida*
Introduced: Introduced in the latter part of the nineteenth century
Description: Fuzzy leaves and brightly colored blossoms characterize this favorite summer annual. The plants are low-growing, reaching a height of only twelve to fifteen inches. Many species are trailing. Blossoms come in almost every color and are either solid or speckled, veined, or striped.

How to grow: Petunia seeds are tiny and dust-like. They should be started indoors ten to twelve weeks before the last frost date. The seeds need light to germinate and should sprout within ten days. In the garden these plants should be spaced eight to ten inches apart in dry, sandy soils. They need full sun.

How to use: Little can compare to the colorful brilliance of petunias planted in a mass. They are good for hanging baskets, bedding plants, and containers.

Original strains of petunias were so uninspiring that the plant was essentially ignored by gardeners for many years. The Indians called it *petun*, or "worthless tobacco." Petunia is, indeed, in the tobacco family. In 1831 another strain was discovered in Argentina, and crossbreeding in the United States developed the garden petunia that is so beloved today.

Common name: PHLOX
Botanical name: *Phlox paniculata*
Introduced: Introduced to colonial gardens during the first part of the eighteenth century
Description: Phlox has lance-shaped leaves and clusters of sweetly scented blossoms ranging in color from white to blue, purple, pink, and red. Each

blossom of this summer perennial has five petals. The plants grow approximately twenty-four to thirty-six inches tall.

How to grow: Phlox needs full sun and rich, well-drained soil. Good air circulation is crucial in the successful cultivation of phlox because mildew is a perennial problem. To prevent mildew, phlox should not be planted next to a rock or brick wall that retains moisture. They should also be spaced far apart and watered from the roots rather than sprinkled from above.

How to use: Phlox adds a sweet smell and lovely colors to the summer garden.

In the language of flowers phlox means sweet dreams or a proposal of love. Leaves from phlox were made into an ointment useful in treating skin disorders. If taken internally, it can ease abdominal pains. Some of the favorite varieties of old-fashioned gardeners were Elizabeth Campbell (salmon pink), Europa (white with a carmine eye), Mrs. Jenkins (white), and the still popular Miss Lingard (white).

Common name: PINCUSHION FLOWER
Botanical name: *Scabiosa caucasica*
Introduced: Introduced during the seventeenth century
Description: This flower grows about two-and-one-half feet tall. Blossoms are nearly three inches across and look like small pincushions surrounded by larger petals. Leaves are long, narrow, and light green. There are relatively few blossoms per plant. Blossoms are white or blue.
How to grow: Pincushion flowers need full sun and should be planted in light, sandy soil. The plants can be divided in spring or planted from seed. They should be spaced eighteen to twenty-four inches apart in the garden. Deadheading the spent blossoms will encourage further flowering.
How to use: Plant pincushion flowers in a mass since they do not bloom prolifically. The blossoms can be used as a cut flower with good results.

John Goodyer, a British gardener and writer, first grew *Scabiosa atropurpurea* in England in 1621. This species was called sweet scabious or mournful widow and was "of a delicate redd colour like to redd velvett." According to the language of flowers this species represented loss and was often used in funeral wreaths in Portugal and Brazil. The current garden species *S. caucasica* was first introduced to English gardens in 1803. It was sometimes called gypsy rose or blackamoor's beauty. Favorite old-fashioned varieties include azure fairy and king-of-the-blacks.

Common name: PORTULACA
Botanical name: *Portulaca grandiflora*
Introduced: Introduced to the colonies between 1700 and 1776
Description: Portulaca is low-growing and creeping. The brightly colored blossoms are available in a variety of colors including pink, red, yellow, cream, orange, and white. Both single and double varieties are available. The leaves are small and needle-like. A great disadvantage to portulaca is that the blossoms close up late in the day. New cultivars have been developed to make the blossoms stay open longer.

How to grow: Portulaca is heat- and drought-tolerant. It likes full sun and thrives during a long, hot summer. Seeds of this annual can be sown after the last spring frost. Blooms should appear approximately eight weeks after sowing. Plants should be thinned ten to twelve inches apart. The plant blooms better on the dry side. Do not overwater.

How to use: Because of its low growth habit, portulaca is good for the rock garden or as a annual ground cover.

A German legend tells why portulaca is also called moss rose. An angel was walking through a forest when she tired and sat down underneath a rose tree to rest. When she woke up, the angel thanked the tree and offered to keep its roots cool by spreading a blanket of moss underneath its branches. This moss bloomed with beautiful bright colors, so today we call it moss rose.

This plant was originally found growing in South America and was taken to Europe in the early 1700s. Although it was originally collected for its beauty and potential as a garden flower, growers soon discovered that the plant had culinary and medicinal value as well. It was used to cure such peculiar ailments as teeth set on edge and gunpowder burns. Portulaca was thought to prevent muscle spasms if held on the neck and believed to prevent thirst if placed under the tongue. The plant has high vitamin content, and its leaves were eaten as a vegetable and used to cure scurvy. Eating portulaca was thought to increase one's appetite. If placed on a child's bed, portulaca was said to keep away evil spirits as the child slept.

Common name: SAXIFRAGE
Botanical name: *Saxifraga stolonifera*
Introduced: Introduced to the U.S. between 1850 and 1900
Description: Saxifrage is a very low-growing perennial with beautifully veined foliage. The leaves are dark green, gently scalloped around the edges, and marked with distinct white veins. The white blossoms measure three-quarters of an inch across. This plant creeps and crawls, rarely getting above twenty-four inches with a spread of twelve to eighteen inches.
How to grow: The plant should be grown in well-drained, fertile soil in light shade. It can be propagated by dividing established plants in the spring. These should be spaced six to nine inches apart.
How to use: Because it is low-growing and likes moist, shady spots, saxifrage is ideal for a rock garden or perhaps as a ground cover under tall evergreens.

The genus name *Saxifraga* means "I break stones." Two possible reasons are given for this name. First is the fact that saxifrage grows in rocky soils and finds its way into cracks and crevices, thus speeding the process of breaking the rocks apart. Another possibility is that saxifrage was at one time considered important for treating gall stones. Other country names include mother of thousands and roving soldier.

Common name: SNAPDRAGON
Botanical name: *Antirrhinum majus*
Introduced: Used in colonial gardens in the early 1700s
Description: Snapdragons are actually perennials grown as annuals. They grow twenty-four to thirty inches tall, though dwarf species are now available. The blossoms have a slightly spicy fragrance and come in a wide variety of bright colors. The flowers have a pouch and lips, thus the name snapdragon. The attractive linear foliage is a bronzy green color.
How to grow: Snapdragons are somewhat tolerant of cold weather and can be set out in the garden about four weeks before the last predicted frost. Seeds can be sown as the soil begins to warm. Do not cover the seeds as they need light to germinate. For best results, plant in full sun in rich, well-drained soil and keep evenly moist.

How to use: Snapdragons are good for the border and annual planting beds. They make very good cut flowers. If spent flower heads are removed, the plants will continue to bloom during the growing season.

The configuration of the flower head has given rise to many descriptive common names, such as toad's mouth, dog's mouth, and lion's mouth. If the blossom is squeezed, it opens to reveal a yawning mouth.

The genus name *Antirrhinum* is from two Greek words: *anti*, meaning "like," and *rhinos*, meaning "snout."

The seeds of snapdragon contain a relatively high percentage of oil. Legend held that he who was annointed with the oil of the snapdragon would become famous. This same oil was thought to hold the power to ward off witchcraft and sorcery.

The blossoms are sometimes used as a dye for cloth.

During the twenties and thirties, rust caused seed production to drop drastically. Researchers at the University of California at Davis found a rustproof snapdragon, which they crossed with a popular garden variety. Repeated crossbreedings finally resulted in disease-free plants and snaps once again took their rightful place in the garden.

Popular older varieties include Keystone and Nelrose, which are pink, Mont Blanc, a white, Golden Queen, yellow, and Moonlight, an apricot and rose color.

Common name: STOCK
Botanical name: *Matthiola incana*
Introduced: Grown in gardens in the colonies during the 1600s
Description: Stock consists of magnificent spikes of cross-shaped flowers. The blossoms can be either single or double; the foliage is an attractive blue-gray. The sweet fragrance is perhaps the most delightful part of the plant, which blooms in spring and grows twenty-four to thirty-six inches tall.
How to grow: This plant likes mild, cool weather and should be set out in mid-spring. They should be spaced twelve to fifteen inches apart in full sun in rich, well-drained soil and should be fertilized once a month while blooming.
How to use: Because of its oustanding fragrance, stock should be grown close to the house in containers on a patio or in planting beds next to a window or deck.

Stock is native to the Isle of Wight. Its name comes from the Latin word *stoce*, meaning "trunk" or "stick," and refers to the straight woody stem of this plant. The genus *Matthiola* was named for Pietro Anderea Matthioli (1501–1577), royal physician to Emperor Maximilian II and author of many papers on medicinal botany. Although he had extensive knowledge of medicinal plants, Matthioli was said to use stock only for "matters of love and lust."

AUTUMN

I liked some parts of my grandma's garden better than others. I liked walking among the flowers pretending to be a princess who never had to work. I didn't like the working, especially during early fall when all the vegetables came in.

Grandma was a firm believer in "Waste not, want not." She used everything that her garden produced and wanted to be sure that her grandchildren learned the importance of putting by for winter. The best way to accomplish that, she figured, was to make us do the putting by. We peeled and snipped and chopped and sieved and stewed and jellied and jammed our way through the fall. In reality we worked only a couple of hours a day, but back then it seemed there was no rest for the weary and that the stream of produce would never end. Every time I thought for sure we were finished, Grandpa would show up at the door, his eyes twinkling and his face wreathed in smiles. "Look at what I found just sitting in the garden waiting for me," he would say. We would groan as he dumped another bushel of pole beans onto the kitchen table.

With a sigh we'd each take a handful and begin the process of stringing the long threads off the beans' sides, snapping the ends off, and breaking every bean into bite-sized pieces. Through the years I got faster and faster at this, but I could never come close to matching Grandma in speed and accuracy. Her fingers flew—she could do a whole fistful of beans while I was still stringing my first.

Like generations of women before us, we sometimes made a game or a party of the work we were doing. Although we soon saw through Grandma's "contests" (Let's see who can string the most beans today!), we did love to see who could find the longest bean or the most peas in a pod or cut the longest continuous apple peel. Every once in a while we would gossip or talk "girl talk." It was around Grandma's big old kitchen table that I first learned the facts of life. And it was there, listening to my grandmother gossip, that I discovered how embellishment makes facts more interesting. My grandmother had a deliciously naughty sense of humor. When she had a really good dirty joke to tell, she would turn to my younger brother and say, "Think your grandpa needs you, boy," and Lee would grin and take off running, glad to be excused from the endless task of canning vegetables. Once he had gone, Grandma would close the door to the kitchen, smile wickedly, and begin, "Did you hear the one about . . ."

A look at Grandma's pantry shelves suggested that she had put by enough each year to feed ten families for ten years. But throughout the winter she and Grandpa would eat beans, tomatoes, corn, squash, peas, and a thousand other things that we had canned. On the pantry shelves she found jars of peaches and string beans for a sick friend. She found a hundred small jars of blackberry jelly to give away at Christmas. She captured all that was good and delicious of summer and doled it out during the cold, drab winter months. These gifts were more than food. They were a little bit of Grandma, captured in a jar.

PUTTING BY

Nothing store-bought compares to the taste of vegetables and fruit right out of the garden. But when summer's long, hot days shorten and the garden turns brown after the first killing frost, fresh produce is no longer a possibility. The next best thing, of course, is to bring out a little bit of that summer produce that's been preserved.

Fruit and vegetable gardens were essential to our ancestors. They were also generous in their bounty. Emma Denton, a gardener from Hiawasee, Georgia, told me that one of her children recently asked if Emma had always had enough to eat while growing up. "Enough to eat!" she exclaimed, and threw up her hands. "Why, there was more to eat than we could possibly put away. All kinds of vegetables and hams and fruit. My daddy had a big orchard of apples and peaches and had enough fruit to feed all of Townes County.

"We used to bleach those apples and peaches with sulphur, and they would last from fall until spring. They were good, too. You could wash them and eat them raw or cook them up and add a little brown sugar.

"Daddy would take dried apples and other vegetables and fruit to markets wherever they were picking cotton. Those folks had money but no fresh fruits and vegetables, and they would buy whatever Daddy would bring. He used to buy our winter clothes with money he made at those markets."

During the peak of harvest, food was delicious and plentiful, not only in the garden but in the wild as well. Sweet, young dandelion greens, collected with the first breath of spring, were tender and delicious. Poke sallet was also considered a spring delicacy. Wild strawberries made into pie or cobbler had no equal. It wasn't necessary to explain how good these dishes were to anyone who tasted them, and it wasn't possible to explain to anyone who had not. Collecting wild fruit was a favorite pastime of the entire family. To gather plums and grapes became known as "plummering" or "grapering."

Sweeteners were made from whatever was handy, including sorghum molasses and boiled-down watermelon juice. In New England, of course, maple sugar was used. On the prairies this was not possible, but resourceful pioneers made their own "maple sugar" from corn cobs. The *Nebraska Pioneer Cookbook* features the following recipe:

> ### *Mock Maple Syrup*
> **1 dozen large, clean red cobs. Cover with water, boil 1 - 2 hours. Drain off water and strain it. There should be a pint of liquid. Add 2 pounds brown sugar and boil to desired thickness.**

Many of the recipes and instructions used in times past are still useful today, for example, these instructions on "Boiling All Kinds of Garden Stuff" found in *The Frugal Colonial Housewife* (1772): "In dressing all sorts of kitchen garden herbs, take care they are clean washed, that there be no small snails or caterpillars between the leaves, and that all the coarse outer leaves and the tops that have received any injury by the weather be taken off. Next wash them in a good deal of water and put them into a cullender to drain. Care must likewise be taken that your pot or sauce-pan be clean, well tinned, and free from sand or grease."

Although food was fresh and plentiful during summer and fall, it took a great deal of work to make sure that there would also be plenty during the winter. Today we can get strawberries in November, watermelon in March, and just about any other kind of fresh produce whenever we want it. Canned and frozen vegetables are available all the time, but our grandmothers did not have this luxury. For many of them, the only winter vegetables available were ones they put up themselves.

In her book *Putting Food By*, Ruth Hertzberg explains that "to put by" is a nineteenth-century way of saying you save something you don't have to use now against the time when you'll need it. She says that putting by is also an antonym for "running scared."

Grandma used many methods of putting by. Probably the most ancient method of food preservation is drying. Later came cooking and smoking, then "potted" foods, where meats and cheeses were immersed in pots of fat or honey. Pickled or fermented foods were submerged in salt or brine. Yesterday's gardener preserved food in a variety of ways. Fruits and vegetables were stored whole in a root cellar. The sweet essence of fruits was captured in jams and jellies. Vegetables were pickled, and both fruits and vegetables were dried in and out of doors.

The Root Cellar

In back of the house, often tucked into a hillside, was the root cellar, which took many different forms. They could be found in hillside caves, garden trenches, and other underground spaces. The root cellar allowed for winter storage without processing. Ideally, a root cellar could hold food for several months after normal harvest time in a cool, moist atmosphere that prevented freezing or decomposing. A root cellar needed to remain between thirty-two and forty degrees Fahrenheit.

Despite its ease and convenience, there are some decided disadvantages to the root cellar that modern gardeners choosing this old-fashioned method should be aware of. Turnips and cabbages often produce strong, unpleasant odors. Some vegetables need higher temperatures than others; for example, squash needs to be kept warmer than carrots. Some fruits and vegetables, such as potatoes and apples, cannot be stored next to each other because of chemical reactions.

Air circulation in the root cellar is important. Produce actually breathes after it has been harvested. Apples are particularly known for this and have been said almost to "pant." This respiration can be modified by layering the produce in clean, dry leaves, sand, moss, or sawdust.

Not all kinds of produce can be successfully stored in a root cellar. Obviously, the best candidates are the root plants such a carrots, onions, turnips, beets, and Irish and sweet potatoes. Other fruits and vegetables that fair well in a root cellar include apples, cabbage,

cauliflower, peppers, and pumpkins.

Some vegetables can be best preserved by leaving them in the ground under a pile of mulch until needed. Parsnips were almost always preserved in this manner. Many thought the taste of this vegetable was actually improved by allowing it to freeze in the ground. In very cold areas it is important to dig parsnips and then heel them into the ground in rows covered with mulch to make them more accessible to the cook.

Onions were dug in late fall, their tops removed, and spread out on the barn floor or in an open shed. They were left there until thoroughly dry, then packed in barrels and put in a cool, dry place. Care was taken to avoid freezing since alternate freezing and thawing causes onions to rot. Onions and garlic were also sometimes braided for storage. To do this, carefully pull the onions, leaving the long stems and leaves attached. Allow them to dry for a few days, then clean the loose dirt off the bulbs. Do not remove the papery outer skin, for this conserves moisture. Place three bulbs on a table with the stems and leaves pointing toward you. Carefully begin braiding the stems, adding other onions as you work your way down. When you have braided together seven onions, tie the stems together with ribbon and hang the bunch up to dry. The length of the braid should be no more than twenty-four inches or it will be too heavy.

Sweet potatoes were stored in bulk. The potatoes were dug before frost and allowed to dry in the sun for a few days. They were then placed in the root cellar or some other cool, dry place on a layer of straw or hay. More straw was piled on top of the layer, then more vegetables on top of the straw. These layers continued, ending with straw. The more sweet potatoes in a pile, the better they kept.

White potatoes were dug when dry then kept out of direct sunlight, which damages their flavor and texture. To keep them from sprouting, potatoes were often soaked in a barrel of water before being dried and stored. Once dried, the potatoes were put in a dark root cellar.

Drying

Drying foods for later use dates back to prehistory and is a method still used throughout the world, particularly in hot, dry areas. Food can be dried outdoors in the sun, in an oven, or in a dark, well-ventilated room. Basically, the drying process removes enough moisture that food does not spoil. In general, drying should be done as rapidly as possible. The produce should be picked in prime condition, peeled, pitted, and cut up. Usually small, thin pieces dry better than larger pieces.

Outdoors, produce was spread on wooden (not metal) trays with slatted or perforated bottoms for good air circulation. Fruits and vegetables that respond best to this method include apples, apricots, cherries, dates, figs, peaches, pears, plumbs, beans, peas, chili (hot) peppers, sweet corn, and sweet potatoes.

Dried apples were a staple for most country gardeners. To dry apples, select late autum varieties, then peel, core, and slice them into one-eighth-inch rings. Coat the slices with a strong ascorbic acid solution to hold color and hang them up to dry.

Apples were sometimes cut into chunks and strung on long pieces of cotton or silk thread. Pumpkins were dried in a different way. The ripe pumpkins were pared and cut into small pieces. These pieces were stewed until soft then mashed through a colander. The resulting pump was spread out on plates about an inch thick and allowed to dry in an oven set on a low temperature. After many hours, the pulp became dry and brittle. These pumpkin sheets were stored in a dry place. When the housewife was ready for a pumpkin pie, she soaked the pieces overnight in milk then used them just as she would fresh pulp.

Canning and Preserving

Canning is a relatively recent means of preserving food that remains enormously popular among gardeners who wish to capture summer's bounty.

Grandma's pantry was not properly stocked unless she had

Spit in my ears
And tell me lies
But give me no
Dried apple pies.
—*Nebraska Pioneer Cookbook*

Leatherbritches Beans
Wash and drain a batch of firm green beans. Remove ends and strings. Use a large darning needle with heavy white thread and thread through the pod near the middle of each, pushing them along the thread so that they are about one-quarter inch apart. Hang up the strings of beans in warm, well-ventilated place to dry. They will shrivel and turn greenish gray. To cook in the winter time, as the pioneers did, cover with water and soak overnight. Drain, renew water, and parboil slowly for a half-hour. Drain again. Cook slowly with ham hock or salt pork until tender. Serve with cornbread. —*Old Timey Recipes*

shelves laden with shiny jars of jams and jellies. These were of every color—deep, clear purple from the grapes, midnight black from blackberries, bright red from cherries, green from mint, pale yellow from apples—creating a rainbow of sweetness. Many of the preserves came from her garden. Another substantial portion, however, was made from wild fruits, adding an almost exotic touch. Such unusual items as dandelions, Queen Anne's lace, and violets were often made into jellies of unusual flavor and delightful color.

Peach Leather
Measure one-half cup of sugar for each pound of peeled, stoned peaches. Put fruit and sugar into a preserving kettle, bring slowly to a boil, and simmer until most of moisture is cooked away, mashing to a smooth paste as they cook. Oil a large china platter, cover with a piece of muslin, and spread the cooked peaches on it in a thin layer. Put the paste in the sun till thoroughly dry, then roll it in the cloth and store in a cool, dry place. To eat, unroll and tear off a piece.—*Nebraska Pioneer Cookbook*

Always make preserves in a porcelain or brass kettle. If the latter, have it scoured first with sand, then with salt and vinegar. Then scald it and put in the sugar and water for the syrup.

In peeling fruit, throw it into cold water to keep it from turning dark, and let it remain there till you are ready to throw it in the boiling syrup. Bear in mind that exposure to the air turns peeled fruit dark. Boil rather quickly. In preserving fruit whole, boil it a short time in the syrup, take it out, let it get cold, and then put it again in the kettle.

Cut sugar is best for preserves which you wish to be clear and light-colored, but nice brown sugar is best for dark-colored jams and marmalades, such as those made of blackberries, raspberries, whortleberries.

— Housekeeping in Old Virginia (1879)

Candied Rose Leaves

Take of the fayrest leaves red or damask and sprinkle them with rose water and lay them one by one on white paper on a hot sunshiney day then beat some double refined sugar very small and sift it thinly on the roses, they will candy as they ly in the hot sun then turne the leaves and strow some rose water on the other side, and sift some sugar in like manner on them, turne them often sometimes strowing on water, and sometimes sifting on sugar till they be enough, then lay them in boxds betwixt clean papers and soe keep them all year. — *The Compleat American Housewife (1776)*

Peach Preserves

Pare and add to a pound of peaches one-and-one-quarter pounds best sugar. Cook very fast for a few moments in a porcelain kettle. Turn out in a bowl, cover with muslin or cambric, set in the sun, stirring every day till the peaches seem quite transparent. They retain their flavor much better this way than when cooked on the fire. Put in jars, cover with paper saturated with brandy, and tie up tightly to exclude the air. — *Housekeeping in Old Virginia (1879)*

Sassafras Jelly

Boil sassafras roots one-half hour and strain. Measure two cups of this tea into pan. Add one package powdered pectin and just barely bring to boil. Add three cups honey (without comb) and two tablespoons of sassafras root bark that has been grated to a fine powder. Simmer six minutes. Put in sterilized glasses and cover with melted paraffin. — *Old Timey Recipes*

Queen Anne's Lace Jelly

Bring to a boil three-and-one-half cups water. Take off heat. Add fifteen large Queen Anne's lace flower heads to make a strong tea. Strain and measure juice. Add one package pectin and one-and-one-quarter cups sugar for every cup of juice used. Boil for one minute and then pour into hot, sterilized jelly jars. Makes four to five cups. — *Shirley Vogler, Talking Rock, Georgia*

Dandelion Blossom Jelly

Pick one quart (packed) dandelion blossoms. Remove stems and all green parts of the flowers. Wash well. Put five cups of water into a saucepan, add blossoms, and bring to a boil. Boil one minute. Strain, reserving liquid. Add one package pectin to liquid. Stir and heat. When liquid boils, add four cups sugar. Simmer until liquid sheets off spoon; then skin and pour into sterilized jars. — *Renee Meyers, Henderson, North Carolina*

Pickles and Relishes

Youngsters gotta chew on something or someone to sharpen their teeth for society. A pickle bites back. When my kids get uppity with me, I tell 'em, "Go get a pickle." — Stillroom Cookery

You need perfect produce to make a perfect pickle. You also need good, strong vinegar. The vinegar should not be boiled because it will lose strength, as will the spices.

Pickled Nasturtium Buds or Seeds

Take the seeds new off the plant when they are pretty large, but before they grow hard, and throw them into the best white wine vinegar that has been boiled up with what spice you please. Keep them close stopped in a bottle. They are fit for use in eight days. — *The Frugal Colonial Housewife* (1772)

Rhubarb Relish

3 cups peeled, sliced rhubarb	**1 teaspoon cinnamon**
1½ cup sugar	**½ teaspoon ground cloves**
½ cup vinegar	

Combine all ingredients and simmer over low heat until smooth and thick, about the consistency of soft jam. Seal in hot jars. Makes one-and-one-half pints. (Rhubarb was used so often in earlier days to make pie that the plant was often called "pie plant.") — *Susan Porter, Alpharetta, Georgia*

Cider and wines

No colonial household was really complete without a few bottles of homemade wine on the shelf and nearly every "receipt" book from this time included recipes for making fruit wines.

Parsnip Wine

For the right flavor this wine must be made in February after the parsnips have been taken out of the ground.

1 quart grated parsnips   **2½ pounds white sugar**
1 gallon boiling water   **¼ teacup liquid yeast**

Put grated parsnips in a stone jar. Pour boiling water over them. Set jar on back of stove where it will keep hot but will not boil. Leave it there four hours. Strain. Wash jar, then return the liquid to it. Add sugar, stir until dissolved. When lukewarm, add yeast. Let stand until seasoned. — *Old Timey Recipes*

Elder-Wine

When the elder-berries are ripe, pick them and put them into a stone jar. Set them in boiling water, or in a slack over, till the jar is as warm as you can well bear to touch it with your hand; then strain the fruit through a coarse cloth, squeezing them hard, and pour the liquor into a kettle. Put it on the fire and let it boil and to every quart of liquor add a pound of Lisbon sugar [soft rather than hard lump or loaf sugar] and scum it often. Then let it settle, and pour it off into a jar and cover it close. — *The Frugal Colonial Housewife* (1772)

CELEBRATIONS

Like most folks in rural areas, Grandma and Grandpa did not have access to much entertainment. Houses were few and far between, and any excuse to get together was pounced upon with great enthusiasm. Planting and harvest time were always good for social gatherings. People would use any excuse to get together, and if work could be accomplished at the same time, all the better. Corn shuckins, pea thrashins, berry stemmins, and apple peelins were all social occasions that truly helped out the host.

In the Appalachian mountains, perhaps the most popular of these was the corn shuckin. Corn from the field would be harvested and brought into the barn yard. All the neighbors were invited, both young and old. Ear after ear of corn would be shucked as stories were told and tales swapped. Sometimes, as an incentive, a bottle of liquor would be buried in the middle of the pile. As Florence Brooks relates in *Foxfire 2,* "We'd shuck all night t'get t'that half-gallon a'liquor. Then we'd all have a drink and probably have a dancin' th'rest a'th'night, if we got done in time."

Sometimes red ears of corn were found. These were called pokeberry corn and held special significance. Sometimes the rule was that whoever found the first red ear of corn got to kiss the prettiest girl. If a girl found it, she got her first pick of dancing partners. Other times, whoever found the first red ear received a prize. The prizes varied from a freshly baked pie to a young calf or a ten-dollar piece.

Harvest time was also fair time. Abraham Lincoln called fairs the "time keeper of history," and with the showing of ageless arts and crafts, livestock, and vegetables, this holds true today. Liberty Hyde Bailey wrote in 1908 that "The fairs should reach all farm children. And the significance of everything at a fair should be explained by a good teacher standing on the spot." Fairs played a large part in the social activities of rural America. They became a time not only to show off the results of hard labor during the growing season, but also to get together, relax, and have a good time at the conclusion of the harvest. Although most state and local fairs today do not hold the significance they once did, these events, especially food festivals, are still popular across the nation.

Among the events that draw crowds and connect us to our past, these are especially interesting:

Pink Tomato Festival, Warren, Arkansas. Bradley County, Arkansas, boasts that it is the "Land of Tall Pines and Pink Tomatoes." Any resident will tell you that the rich, loamy soil in this part of the country grows the best tomatoes in the world. Why are they pink? If left on the vine, they would eventually become as red as tomatoes from California or Florida, but Arkansas tomatoes are picked when they first turn red and shipped all over the country.

The first Pink Tomato Festival was held in 1956. Today the festival draws seventy thousand participants annually, and they really "paint the town pink." Activities include tomato eating contests, a tomato toss, and tomato bobbing.

The National Asparagus Festival is jointly sponsored and hosted by Shelby and Hart, Michigan. The slogan for the festival is "every inch edible," for asparagus here is harvested by hand. There is no tough white part left on the stem and the entire stalk can be eaten. Michigan asparagus is said to be particularly good because the soil is light and sandy, giving the root or crown plenty of oxygen. In this part of the country about twelve thousand acres are planted in asparagus, with harvest lasting about six weeks. Food at the festival includes asparagus bread, fried asparagus, and asparagus soup.

The Ipswich Strawberry Festival is held in Ipswich, Massachusetts. Begun as a church fundraiser in 1935, the festival is known for selling "anything you can make from a strawberry," including shortcake, pie, ice cream, sundaes, jams, tarts, punch, turnovers, and milkshakes. Ipswich strawberries are small and very flavorful.

The Watermelon Festival in Hope, Arkansas, spotlights the area's truly awesome melons. In 1925 the Laseter brothers produced a watermelon weighing 136 pounds; they sent it to President Calvin Coolidge. Continuing this tradition, in 1979 Lloyd and Ivan Bright raised a two-hundred-pound melon that holds the record in the *Guinness Book of World Records.*

The Watermelon Festival—"a slice of the good life"—was first held in Hope in 1926. The mid-August events include a watermelon-eating contest (the announcer assures the contestants "don't worry about the seeds; they come out tomorrow") and a seed-spitting contest in which winners have spit up to twelve feet.

The **Circleville Pumpkin Show** has been held in Circleville, Ohio, since 1903. It is billed as the "Greatest Free Show on Earth." Folks in Circleville really go in for size. One year they baked the world's largest pumpkin pie, which was five feet in diameter and weighed 350 pounds. Another year they had the biggest pumpkin, 385 pounds. How do they grow such large pumpkins in Circleville? The secret is, farmers from the area assure you, plenty of water and TLC.

The **Okra Strut** is held annually in Irmo, South Carolina, and includes an okra-eating contest called the Shoot-out at the Okra

Corral. Due to the sliminess of boiled okra, this is not always the most popular contest. One contestant complained that he "ate so much boiled okra when I was a boy that I couldn't keep my socks up."

The **International Zucchini Festival** is held in Harrisville, New Hampshire. The thirty-two different contests held during the festival include longest or heaviest zucchini competition, a zucchini look-alike contest, the best off-color zucchini award, and the farthest-traveled zucchini prize. A zucchini regatta, with prizes for the zuke that sinks fastest and that stays afloat the longest, is also featured.

The festivities include a zucchini poetry contest. E. A. Caldwell won the 1983 contest with the following poem:

The Uses of Zucchini

I wrote an ode to a vegetable greeny
The lowly, tasteless, common zucchini.
The survival of this hardy garden species
Requires no lime or pesticides or cow feces.
The prolific vines of this family of squash
Will produce in the desert, bog or marsh.
Much like kudzu in a Georgia patch,
The fecundity of this plant is hard to match.

And as soon as these vines begin to produce
We eat zucchini casseroles, bread, and mousse.
Zucchini on granola, ice cream, and pies
A zucchini facial to relax the eyes.
Zucchini daiquiris give a change of pace
To zucchini pickles and soup base.
We try zucchini jellies, jam and juice
And zucchini stuffing for our Christmas goose.

We're served zucchini doughnuts, fried zucchini.
We eat it raw and marinated in linguini.
On resaurant menus are zucchanoes.
But here's an idea we'd be wise to use
We could get zucchinis growing on the global scene
With an Agricultural / Industrial Zucchini Machine.
To show we care for kids and dads and moms
We could stockpile zucchini instead of bombs.

Other annual events include hundreds of apple festivals throughout the country, a cranberry festival in South Carver, Massachusetts, the Vidalia Onion Festival in Vidalia, Georgia, and the Blueberry Festival in Union, Maine, where they grow "fog-nourished blueberries."

TYPICAL AUTUMN PLANTS FROM GRANDMA'S GARDEN

Common Name: AGERATUM

Botanical name: *Ageratum* sp.

Introduced: Dwarf blue ageratum introduced between 1850 and 1900

Description: A small, compact annual, ageratum has small powder-puff-like blossoms that usually come in shades of blue, purple, and pink. Hybrid plants vary in height from five to twenty-four inches. Leaves are small, scalloped on the edges, and oval-shaped.

How to grow: Ageratums grow easily from seed. Plant seeds indoors six to eight weeks before the last frost date and set plants out six to eight inches apart in well-drained, rich garden soil. Ageratums do best with consistently moist soil and feedings of 5-10-5 fertilizer once a month during the **growing** season.

How to use: Newer low-growing hybrids are useful as bedding plants. Fall-blooming varieties look particularly good when planted with various shades of chrysanthemums.

Ageratums have always been useful in the garden because their flowers fade so gracefully. The name is from two Greek words: *a* meaning "not," and *geras,* meaning "old." Taken together, the name indicates that the plant never looks old or bedraggled. A folk superstition holds that those who ate the plant would never get old. A common name for ageratum is floss flower. Favorite old-fashioned varieties include Cope's pet, a lilac color, and blue perfection.

Anemone japonica alba

Common Name: ANEMONE
Botanical name: *Anemone coronaria*
Introduced: Tuberous anemones introduced during the 1700s; *Anemone pulsatilla,* or pasque flower (wind flower or Emanies), used in colonial gardens
Description: The genus *Anemone* contains many species. Favorite garden varieties generally grow from a tuber. The foliage is soft, finely dissected, and

fern-like. Blossoms resemble either a daisy or a poppy and are borne on single stems that grow approximately ten to eighteen inches tall. At night and during cloudy weather the blossoms close up. *Anemone coronaria* has poppy-like flowers measuring one to two-and-one-half inches across. Flower colors include red, purple, white, and blue. The species *A. japonica,* popular during the early twentieth century, was brought from China in the 1850s by Robert Fortune.

How to grow: The tubers, which look like small pieces of bark, should be soaked overnight in warm water before being planted. Plant in fall in well-drained soil rich in organic matter. These plants need filtered sunlight but can be grown in full sun in mild regions.

How to use: Different species of anemones will bloom in early spring, early summer, or fall. The bright colors from this plant are welcomed in spring when so many flowers show only pastel colors.

Anemones have been a garden fixture for many centuries. The species *A. pavonina* was grown in Europe as early as the sixteenth century and was very popular during both the seventeenth and eighteenth centuries. Late in the seventeenth century forms were developed with broad petals surrounding a mass of colored filaments. Such forms are called "anemone-flowered" and include peonies, dahlias, and other similarly structured plants.

The single or semi-double *A. coronaria* were very popular in England. From France double varieties known as St. Brigid anemones were formed and used for spring and early summer bedding flowers.

The name is from the Greek word for "wind"; in many areas the plant is called wind flower. According to a Greek legend about the origin of the plant, Anemone was a nymph loved by the god of the west wind, Zephyr. Zephyr, in turn, was loved by Flora, goddess of flowers. Because Zephyr did not return her love, Flora became jealous and changed the nymph into a flower. Zephyr did not particularly like anemone as a flower and soon abandoned her to the love of the god of the north wind, Boreas. Legend says whenever the wind blows from the north, anemones bend gently in greeting. Pliny, the Roman writer and statesman, said that anemones would open only at the bidding of the wind.

Because of the close association of anemones, wind, and air, the plant became synonomous with the breath of life. The name also has links to the Sanskrit word *anti,* meaning "he breathes." In many early European communities, rural folks would hold their breath as they ran past a field of anemones, for they believed that the plant poisoned the air with disease.

Common name: ASTER

Botanical name: *Aster frikartii*

Introduced: Native to the U.S.; first used in colonial gardens during the seventeenth century

Description: Of the hundreds of asters native to the United States, one of the most popular garden species is *Aster frikartii.* This aster has small, fragrant, lavender-blue flowers that look like small daisies with an attractive yellow center. The plants grow two to three feet tall and bloom from early summer through fall. Varieties of the New England aster (*Aster novae-angliae*) are also popular, though these generally grow taller than *A. friktarii.*

How to grow: Asters like full sun and well-drained, rich soil. It is easy to propagate asters by dividing the plants every three to four years and using the outside portions of the clump. New plants can be set out in spring or fall and should be spaced two to three feet apart.

How to use: Asters are useful in the fall perennial garden. Taller varieties can be put at the back of a border. Native strains can be used in a more naturalized setting or in a wildflower garden.

A. novae-angliae and *A. novae-belgii* have undergone the most intensive breeding and hybridization.

Asters have been known for many centuries and were considered sacred to both Greek and Roman gods and goddesses. The word *aster* comes from the Latin word for star. According to legend, asters were created when Virgo, looking down from heaven, sprinkled stardust on the earth and the fields bloomed with asters. Another story tells of the goddess Asterea, who looked down on earth and saw no stars. It was such a sad sight that she began to cry. Where her tears fell, asters bloomed.

The Greeks believed asters held magical powers. Leaves from the plants were burned to keep away evil spirits, serpents, and snakes. In England the plant, known as starwort, was chosen as the floral emblem for September. In France it was called eye of Christ.

Aster amellus is native to southern Europe and was grown in Roman time. It became an important garden plant during the seventeenth century. In its native form flowers occur in red, white, and blue. After World War I the hybrid King George was very popular in England.

Common name: CALENDULA
Botanical name: *Calendula officinalis*
Introduced: Brought to the U.S. in the early 1600s
Description: Calendula has bright yellow or orangish daisy-like blossoms that close by early evening. The plant is multi-branched and grows to a height of eighteen to twenty-four inches, spreading nearly twenty-four inches across. The oblong leaves have smooth edges, and the entire plant is covered with tiny hairs. When bruised, the plant gives off a slightly medicinal odor. This annual blooms best during cool weather in the spring and fall.
How to grow: Because calendula blooms best at cooler temperatures, it is often used as a fall bedding plant. Calendula comes easily from seeds but has a short life span. Use fresh seeds and sow outdoors in late spring, approximately one-half inch deep. Germination requires total darkness with soil covering all seeds. Once the seeds have germinated, the plants need full sun but are relatively tolerant of infertile soils. Keep the seedlings free of weeds and thin to approximately ten to twelve inches apart.
How to use: Calendulas make a very nice fall bedding plant. Their color and fragrance are welcome additions to the garden. Plant breeders have developed larger and fuller strains from the original old-fashioned variety. The plant can be used in herb or ornamental gardens. It was often included in the kitchen garden for its beauty and culinary value.

Although calendula is most often listed as an herb, the bright yellow flowers have earned a niche in the formal garden as well. Historically, calendula has been called marigold, or pot marigold. In the late 1600s the poet John Gay posed the riddle: "What flower is that which bears the Virgin's name, / The richest metal joined to the same?" Although his answer was marigold, he meant calendula, not the small plant of the genus *Tagetes* that we usually think of as marigold. Calendula was used to cure many different ailments including toothaches, skin irritations, measles, varicose veins, and ulcers. Taken with wine it was thought to soothe a "cold stomach."

During the thirteenth and fourteenth centuries calendula was grown widely as a cheap substitute for saffron. A cordial made from calendula was used to treat depression. During the late sixteenth century double varieties were popular. John Gerard wrote of cultivating calendulas for a color that was like "pure gold." Single varieties regained favor in eighteenth-century herb gardens and were used as flavoring. Old-fashioned varieties include Lemon King and Nankeen, which were light yellow, and Orange King, a deep orange color.

Common name: CHRYSANTHEMUM
Botanical name: *Chrysanthemum* sp.
Introduced: Japanese and Chinese chrysanthemums introduced to the U.S. between 1850 and 1900; *Chrysanthemum leucanthemun,* the common ox-eye daisy, used in North American gardens during the seventeenth century
Description: Tremendous variety exists within this genus. *C.* x *morifolium* is considered the florists' chrysanthemum. Varieties within this species are divided into six different groups. These are cushion, daisy, decorative, pompom, spider, and spoon. Older categories were easier. These included pompoms (such as golden climax, Julia, Western beauty, and Rena), single

(Glorianna, Portia, and Yvonne) and double (Rosea, Lillian Doty, Cranfordia, and Mrs. Vincent.) *C. morifolium* is a hybrid developed from four species native to Asia. Chrysanthemums feature every imaginable flower shape with ferny, scented foliage and blooms of every color except blue.

How to grow: Good conditions for growing chrysanthemums include full sun and rich, well-drained soil. Careful pruning during summer months wili result in larger blooms in autumn. Pinch back new plants beginning when they are about six inches tall and continue to do so until ninety days before they bloom. Chrysanthemums are heavy feeders and should be treated to applications of liquid manure weekly during the growing season.

Records indicate that chrysanthemums are among the oldest known cultivated plants. Confucious wrote of them in 500 B.C. Chrysanthemus have always been special in Asia. In 910 A.D. Japan declared the chrysanthemum its national flower and held the first Imperial Chrysanthemum Show. The floral emblem on Japan's coat of arms is probably based on a sixteen-petaled golden chrysanthemum.

Although chrysanthemums were first introduced to European gardeners in 1688, they were virtually ignored for many years. In 1843, however, Robert Fortune went to China and brought back with him the autumn flowering chrysanthemums, a beautiful species that sparked interest in the entire genus. Chrysanthemums, especially the small button variety, were very popular in France. They were called pompons because they so closely resembled the small wool pompons on soldiers' hats.

New varieties of chrysanthemums, sent directly from China, arrived in England early in the nineteenth century. By 1834 many different types were available, including singles, doubles, quilled, and ranunculus-flowered varieties. Colors ranged from rose, salmon, and pink to yellow and white.

An 1846 chrysanthemum show in England brought to fame a Mr. Bowler of Ipswich, who won all the ribbons with his prized chrysanthemum. This particular plant was reported to be twenty-seven feet in circumference and to hold more than a thousand flowers.

Chrysanthemums were brought to this country in the late eighteenth century; in 1900 the Chrysanthemum Society of America was established.

WINTER

One of my most prized possessions is a letter I received from my grandmother several years before she died. This letter spoke to my heart, and after sharing it with my mother and sisters, I lovingly put it in my treasure chest to share with my children when they got old enough.

January 11

Dear Laura,

I hope that this finds you well and happy. Your grandpa and I are doing fine, but it sure is cold. The ground is icy and the wind is so cold that we only leave our warm chairs long enough to walk to the mailbox and back.

You wouldn't recognize your flower garden now. It is all barren and desolate and there's not a flower to be seen. The birds don't seem to mind, though, they still come and nibble at the big old sunflower seeds still standing by the back fence and chirp and carry on just like it's springtime.

It didn't take them long to strip away all the leftover seeds so I made your grandpa go out and fill up all the bird feeders a few days ago. It took all the little birds a while to find them, but now it's like a convention out there every day. We have such fun watching them. Grandpa pretends that he doesn't really care, but he'll stand and watch them for an hour at a time. I asked him why he didn't sit down and he said that he didn't have time to sit and watch a bunch of silly birds. I guess he just has time to stand and watch them!

Don't think that there's nothing going on in our garden just because you can't see anything. All those plants we put out in the fall are snuggling down into their new homes and by spring they will be ready to take off and grow.

You have to have faith to garden, faith that it will rain, that the sun will shine, that the seeds will sprout, and that everything will survive the cold winter. I know that if it gets much colder not all of our plants will make it through, but I have faith that most of them will.

And I guess that's what I love so much about gardening. There are no guarantees. No one can stand here and say, yes, if you plant this seed you will have twelve flowers by July. No one can make that promise. You do what you can to help out Mother Nature, and the rest of it is just left to fate, and you have to have faith that spring will come again and that the garden will turn back into that fairyland that you love so much.

The good Lord says that for every thing there is a season, and for the garden this is the season for rest. For us, this is the season for faith.

Love,
Grandma

SEED CATALOGUES AND ALMANACS

From January until April Grandma's bedside table was laden with seed and feed catalogues from practically every mail-order nursery in the country. The long, dreary months of winter bloomed for Grandma in a happy haze of garden dreams. Perhaps the garden never looked so good as it did in her winter dreaming, inspired by the catalogues and uncluttered by reality.

Grandma's seed catalogue craze could be divided into three distinct phases: dreaming, comparing, and ordering. Her favorite stage, and mine, too, of course, was the dreaming phase. Then anything was possible—size and budget were of no consequence. We talked of redoing the entire front garden, of putting in a whole new rose garden on the east side of the house. We dreamed of putting in a three-acre wildflower meadow and a bog garden down by the creek. We discussed at length the virtues of the new seed introductions and new hybrid strains. We argued about the desirability of a white marigold or a seedless watermelon. Through it all, we laughed and carried on as only dreamers can.

Eventually, though, we began to bring a little reality into our dreaming. Perhaps, we told each other, we should consider just how much all these seeds would cost. "They're just seeds, Grandma, and seeds are cheap," I told her, but she insisted that we begin to figure on paper. We each made out our dream list and at the end added up the total. Grandma's came to $979.53, mine a more sedate $893.67.

"Better than last year," Grandma remarked dryly.

So we began again, this time with a budget in mind. We narrowed down the number of catalogues to a mere half-dozen and started comparing prices, sizes of plants, and number of seeds. It was a tedious but fascinating process of which we never tired.

Finally, afer months of work and play, we were ready to fill out the order forms. Our original dream list had shrunk to the reality of our budget. We had to give up the bog garden, but we did decide to plant a quarter-acre in wildflower seeds. We always included the old standbys: zinnias, impatiens, globe amaranths, hollyhocks, four o'clocks, and dahlias—along with a smattering of new things. After all, we had to keep up with the times, Grandma said. By March 1, the forms had all been filled out, the checks signed, and we sent them off. But I went to the mailbox with a bittersweet feeling, knowing that half the fun was getting there.

In the dead of winter, seed catalogues brought the same joy and temptation to homes throughout the country that we experienced in Grandma's kitchen. Even today when the number of glossy catalogues coming through the mail is enough to stagger even the most stalwart mail carrier, the arrival of these spring promises brightens the day of any gardener.

January is a dead season, when one cannot get out to do anything active in the garden, so one is reduced to studying catalogues under the lamp and thereby being induced to order far more plants or seeds than one ought to. —*Sackville-West*

126

This catalogue lure is an old one, but it is a perennial surprise that I should never acquire immunity to it. —*James McFarland,* My Growing Garden

127

Mail orders, or at least long-distance purchase of seeds and plants, were a necessity for the early colonists. They realized early on that their new home could not supply them with many of the plants that they wished to grow. So back to England, or Scotland, or Germany, or France they wrote, asking friends and acquaintances to send packages of seeds. Soon, as the number of requests increased, this practice became big business. Records show that in 1631 John Winthrop, Jr., of the Massachusetts Bay Colony received from England seeds for fifty-nine kinds of herbs, vegetables, and flowers — all of which cost him about sixteen days' worth of wages for approximately seven-and-one-half pounds of seeds.

Soon enterprising colonists were collecting seeds for themselves and to sell to others. Many of these came from native American plants. In 1783 John Bartram published one of the country's first nursery catalogues, advertising a stock of native plants. Although the list was rather impressive for the times, offering more than two hundred different plants, the catalogue itself was rather stark: merely a list of names, common and botanical, on a single sheet of heavy paper. The only additional information was recommended soil types for each plant.

"You Can't *Buy* Apples Like These
*You Must Grow Them Yourself
—and Gee! They Taste Bully*"

The first real American catalogue was devised and designed by Joseph Breck, founder of a seed company still in business today. In 1840 Breck published the New England Agricultural Warehouse and Seed Store Catalogue, a book of eighty-four pages and seventy-two black-and-white engravings. Breck's use of drawings was innovative and unusual for his time. He was unceasing in his efforts to educate his customers. In addition to information about the plants and their cultural needs, the catalogue included pages of essays and stories of a horticultural appeal.

In 1864 James Vick added a vibrant touch to nursery catalogues by including color. He featured a full-page color picture of the double zinnia, then the pet of the gardening world. Although Vick had no better plants than his competitors, his wise use of illustrations and his chatty, personal writing style made his catalogue extremely popular.

During the last half of the 1800s many outstanding nurserymen developed catalogues that became national bestsellers. Peter Henderson and Luther Burbank were two, but the most outstanding was W. Atlee Burpee. He began in 1876 with a small forty-eight-page publication. At this time the greatest portion of his business was done in poultry and livestock. But by 1915 he sold only seeds, and his catalogue was more than two hundred pages long.

All these nurserymen spent enormous time and energy to produce the best catalogues possible. Much of the energy was devoted to developing friendships, through correspondence, with customers. Letters were important to their buyers and, as always, gardeners had a lot to say to each other.

ALMANACS

Long before seed catalogues were available to aid the gardener in knowing when and what to plant, almanacs filled this need. Almanacs were among America's first printed books, originating in Cambridge or Boston in the seventeenth century. These little volumes of folklore and humor also contained important agricultural information, household hints, weather predictions, and recipes for home remedies. According to Sharon Cosner's article on almanacs in *Americana* magazine, these early how-to books were the "forerunners of cookbooks, calendars, timetables and maps, diaries, joke books, astronomical, astrological, and medical journals."

The seventeenth and eighteenth centuries saw a tremendous increase in the popularity of almanacs. More were printed in America during this era than any other kind of book, with the libraries of many families, particularly on the frontier, consisting of only the Bible and an almanac.

An important part of every almanac was information on planting by the moon and predicting the weather. Their editors and publishers were thought to possess magical gifts in weather prophesy, or so it often seemed. The story is told of an almanac editor who forgot to put in a weather prediction for July 13. At the last minute he instructed his apprentice to fill in a prediction. The young boy wrote in that it would hail, rain, and snow on that day. To the amazement of all (including the apprentice) it did indeed rain, snow, and hail on July 13 of that year.

The *Old Farmer's Almanac,* still published today, was first printed in 1793 by Robert B. Thomas. In 1806 he was joined by Abraham Weatherwise, who had his own formulas for predicting the weather. His predictions were amazingly accurate, some years as high as 85 percent correct.

By the late 1800s the almanac craze had peaked in this country. During the last years of the nineteenth century advertisements for patent medicines were printed in them and reached willing and gullible customers by the thousands, thus the almanacs became more objects of curiosity than sage and informative journals.

HOME REMEDIES FROM THE GARDEN

Grandma was always in search of a guinea pig. She loved playing with her herbs, making concoctions and decoctions, syrups and infusions from the multitude of herbal plants she grew. Although she was busy outdoors with her flowers and vegetable garden in summer and fall, her winter days were happily spent inside stirring, tasting, and perfecting medicines for every possible hurt or ailment.

This was (coincidentally) the same time that colds and fevers usually caught up with Grandma's many friends and grandchildren.

Grandma herself was unfairly healthy and free of physical complaint. While the rest of us sniffled and coughed our way through January and February, she dashed from one bedside to another, trying this or that and taking copious notes on the results. She loved her role as a good witch, of sorts, a twentieth-century herb woman. Not all of her patients, myself included, were as enthusiastic as Grandma about her remedies.

Her favorite—and our most dreaded—was tansy tea. It had the most bitter taste of anything I've ever put in my mouth. But it certainly stopped our coughing. I often chose to stifle my cough rather than be subjected to Grandma's tansy tea. All in all, Grandma's remedies were generally harmless, and some of them were probably quite helpful. But I suspect it was Grandma's energy, love, and eternal optimism, not the herbs themselves, that really made us feel better.

Throughout history, housewives have used their gardens to supply essential medicines for the home. The first colonists relied on a variety of sources to cure their illnesses. They had been able to bring with them only a small number of plants and healing herbs, which they carefully and lovingly planted in their new home. Some flourished and supplied much needed medicine to the settlers. Others did not adapt well to their new home or were so dried out from the long voyage that they were not worth planting.

The colonists wrote home to friends and family begging for more seeds and plants, and eventually these requests were granted, resulting in flourishing herb gardens in many communities. Some of the favorite healing herbs from colonial days include alehoof (ground ivy), garlic, elder, sage, rue, saffron, tansy, wormwood, comfrey, yarrow, chamomile, mint, and dill. In 1686 it was written of a Dr. Bullvant that "He does not direct his patients to the East Indies to look for drugs when they may have far better out of their own gardens."

While settlers were waiting for plants to arrive from Europe, they had to find other sources for medicines. They turned to the woods and fields surrounding their homes. The plants they used were chosen on the basis of two criteria: they closely resembled wild medicinal plants from their former homes, or friendly Indians passed on their knowledge and understanding of the wild plants that grew in America.

The Indians believed that all illness could be traced to an imbalance in the body related to some physical or spiritual act. Healing was accomplished through a combination of herbal remedies and spiritual rituals. Many tribes believed that secrets of healing were revealed in dreams, and the shamen, or medicine men and women of the tribe, would spend days in a self-induced hallucinogenic state in order to penetrate medicine's secrets. Some of the more commonly used Indian medicinal plants include Joe-pye weed, goldenseal, mayapple, sassafras, witch hazel, and American ginseng.

Most housewives, and doctors too, took great pride in preparing their own home remedies. For example, the "water of life" was given as a tonic and to reduce a fever. It was made from balm leaves and stalks, betony leaves and flowers, rosemary, red sage, tarragon, roses, carnation, thyme, and red mint. All of this had to be beaten together and covered with white wine then steeped for eight days before it was ready for use.

Some of the ingredients in herbal remedies were a bit hard to come by. For example, one old recipe reads: "Take juice from Damask Rose and mix with powders of amber, pearl, rubies, of each half a dram." Another recipe called for unicorns' horns ground into powder.

The dosage of many of these old-fashioned remedies was a little vague. Measurements included the following: enough to lie on a pen knife's point; weight of a shilling; enough to cover a French crown; as great as a charger; a little handful; a pretty draught.

Some of the complaints of days past were quite different from today's ailments. The plague was, of course, dreaded. One recipe suggested that "Angelica roots and wine vinegar, if taken while fasting,

To preserve aromatic and other herbs: the boxes and drawers in which vegetable matters are kept should not impart to them any smell or taste. — *Family Receipt Book (1891)*

your breath would kill the plague." Another common ailment was a "cold stomack." A sure cure for this was a "restorative bag" of herbs heated in "boyl'd vinegar," according to *Miss Leslie's Complete Cookery,* published in 1839.

The harvesting and preserving of herbs was of crucial importance, for if harvested at the wrong time or stored improperly, their medicinal value would be negligible.

While fresh herbs are generally preferred for cooking, dried herbs have more concentrated ingredients and are better for medicinal purposes. To dry medicinal herbs, cut stalks and hang upside down in a dark, well-ventilated place. For heavy material, such as roots and heavy stems, clean thoroughly, chop up, and allow to dry. Place the dried material in clean glass jars for storage. Grinding or crushing releases essential plant oils and should not be done until the herb treatment is needed.

Dried herbs should be stored in containers that will not add to nor detract from the potency of the plant itself. Today we have many suitable containers available, including opaque glass, wood, or hard plastic. Stored herbs should be kept in a cool, dry, dark place.

There were many different kinds of herbal medicines. These included distilled waters, teas, infusions, syrups, juleps, decoctions, oils, electuaries, conserves, preserves, lohocks, ointments, plasters, poultices, troches, and pills.

Teas — The most common form of herbal medicine is teas made from leaves, flowers, or sometimes barks of certain plants. A general rule of thumb for medicinal tea is one ounce of plant material to one pint of water, brewed for three to five minutes.

Infusions — These are stronger than teas and generally made in larger quantities to be taken over a day's time. Infusions are brewed fifteen minutes to several hours, then bottled. One-half cup three times during the day is the usual dosage.

Syrups — Honey is usually the base for herb syrups. Add two to three tablespoons of dried herbs to one quart of distilled water. Boil this down to about half and add two tablespoons of honey to two to three tablespoons of herb water. Store in a glass jar in the refrigerator. The syrup will last up to one month.

Poultices — Poultices are used to draw out infections or to relieve pain from muscle strain or spasms. They are made from dried herbs that have been ground or powdered. Mixed with hot water or herbal tea and thickened with oatmeal or flour, the poultices are smeared on the skin and covered with warm, damp towels or cloths.

The following remedies are offered for interest and information. Many garden plants are poisonous and should not be taken internally. Be sure of the identity of any plant you use. Also be aware that many

By drying herbs with artificial heat as quickly as possible, you preserve their scent and flavour much better than when they are dried slowly by exposing them to the sun and air. — *Miss Leslie's Complete Cookery (1839)*

people have allergic reactions to different herbs. If you are using an herb for the first time, take small doses at first. It is best to consult with a physician if treating yourself for any ailment. But many of these remedies were good enough for Grandma, and many are still useful today. Some are quaint superstitions; some are serious, effective remedies.

Common Cold
Wear a clove of garlic around your neck.
For sinuses, put several drops of peppermint oil into a pan of hot
  water. Breathe the vapors through your mouth and nostrils.
Drink mullein tea for chest colds, bronchitis, and asthma.
Drink tea from the California poppy or feverfew.
Eat garlic.
Eat horseradish; rub goose grease on your chest; eat chicken soup.

Sore Throat
Treat with inner bark of slippery elm, dried and pounded into powder.
Drink red clover tea or sage tea with honey.
Mix the pulp of roasted apples with an ounce of tobacco, then wet the
  whole with spirits of wine, spread on a linen rag, and bind to the
  throat.
Boil sage, rosemary, honeysuckle, and plantain in water and wine with
  some honey. Use to wash cankers and sore mouths and throats.
Make mouthwash from lavender blossoms.

Coughs
Poppy blossoms and seeds make a good children's cough syrup.
Drink thyme tea for spasms and cough.
Use hollyhock cough syrup.
Use comfrey for whooping cough in children.
Try a mullein plaster as a decongestant.
Cook saffron in meat to treat asthma.
Try peppermint oil mixed with water and white sugar for asthma.

Colic in Infants
Alder tea is good for colic, but its stain will never come out of clothes.
Make a broth from summer savory.
Give catnip tea or ground ivy tea sweetened with honey.
Tansy tea is also good.

Earaches

Winter savory heated with oil of roses and dropped in the ear can
remove noise and singing in the ear and deafness.

Steam the head over hot herbs, bathe the feet, and put into the ear
cotton wool wet and sweet oil and paregoric. (*The Way to Live Well
and to Be Well While We Live* [1849]).

Treat with oil from mullein.

Headaches

Use thyme to strengthen the brain.

Wear a cabbage leaf in your hat.

Drink tea made from basil, catnip, chamomile, passionflower, mint,
rosemary.

To keep from getting migraine headaches, eat three to four small
feverfew leaves daily. Because the taste is bitter, this can be mixed
with other food.

Gilloflower Syrup for Headaches
Pick three pounds of blossoms
from carnations, sweet William,
or other pinks. Remove from
husks and cut off white heels.
Pour over five pints boiling
water. Let stand twelve hours,
strain off clear liquor, and
dissolve in it two pounds of sugar
to every pint. —*Family Herball*
(1812)

Insect Bites and Stings

Eat delphinium seeds for head lice.

Try a poultice from hollyhock for insect bites.

Carry an onion in your pocket when you go hiking. Also carry strips
of an old bedsheet. When you get bitten or stung, tie a piece of
onion on the bite. The skin turns green, but it works.

Use comfrey leaves, mashed and added to water, for insect bites.

Lay fresh mint leaves on insect bites.

Place a plantain leaf on stings and bites.

Cuts and Bruises

Use sage lotion or marigolds for cuts.

Chervil will take down swelling on bruises.

Try a soft poultice of stewed white beans, put on in a thin muslin bag
and renewed every hour or two, for swelling.

Use a compress of comfrey leaves and root for bruises, swelling,
sprains, and boils. Chop fresh leaves and mix with boiling water.
After cooling, put between layers of cheesecloth and apply as a
poultice.

Tansy leaves pounded with a little spirits are good for bruises.

Apply sage tea to cuts.

Mistletoe leaves and wax made into a salve helps sores.

Skin Disorders

Rub goldenseal on sores.

Drink primrose water for smooth, wrinkle-free skin.

Try pansy tea, taken internally or as a lotion, for skin problems.

Witch hazel bark, twigs, and leaves mixed with alcohol and water
makes a good astringent.

Comfrey brings boils to a head.

For blisters, scrape two carrots and stew in two tablespoons of hog's lard. Add two plantain leaves. When the carrots are well done, strain and apply to blisters.

Take okra blooms, beat them to a pulp, and put them on a boil. It will come to a head in four to five days and will get well.

For poison ivy take plantain leaves, rub them between your fingers, and apply the crushed leaves to the rash from poison ivy.

For poison ivy extract the juice from jewelweed. Freeze it in ice cube trays, and apply when needed.

Drink sassafras tea for poison ivy.

Treat pimples with comfrey leaves.

Warts

Rub marigold blossoms over warts.

Make an infusion from bruised phlox and campanula leaves. Rub on warts. Repeat three to four times.

Rub with a grain of corn. Then feed the corn to a rooster.

Rub with a potato peel and bury the peel. (Anyone who digs up the peel will get the warts.)

Rub beans over the warts and say "Hocus-pocus, presto-change."

Rub with onion juice and vinegar.

Canker Sores and Mouth Ulcers

Chew green strawberry leaves or the root of wild geranium.

Swish a decoction of blackberry leaves sweetened with honey in the mouth.

Violet leaves and blossoms make a slimy tea good for canker sores.

Drink tea made from sage, rosemary, honeysuckle, or plantain.

Toothaches

Drink catnip tea, rosewater, saffron tea.

Try marjoram tea.

Two spoonsful of distilled water from lavender flowers taken orally should ease pain.

Use a poultice from ginger or common chickweed.

Brush your teeth with comfrey root.

Rheumatism and Arthritis

Drink alfalfa or candytuft tea.

Apply verbena leaves boiled in vinegar.

Apply dried leaves of sweet marjoram soaked in flannel bag in boiling water.

For arthritis attach a potato to the affected part of the body and go to bed with a piece of potato in each hand.

For rheumatism, inhale the odor from dry rose leaves on a smoldering fire.

Drink dandelion tea every morning and every evening.

Nervous Disorders and Heart Disease

Take foxglove. (Be careful: this is poisonous in incorrect amounts.)

Drink tea made from lily of the valley flowers. (Be careful: this is poisonous in incorrect amounts.)

For epilepsy take the center purple floret from Queen Anne's lace.

Blood Disorders

Drink garlic tea for high blood pressure and to lower cholesterol.

Violets purify the blood.

Lesser periwinkle reduces blood pressure.

"Ashes of rosemary burnt doth fassen loose teeth and beautifieth the same if they be rubbed there with." — *Eighteenth-century herbal*

"A conserve of sage flowers eaten to warm and comfort the Brain and Nerves, to help and restore the memory, quicken the Senses." — *Botanologia, the English Herbal (1710)*

For epilepsy: "Procure the fresh root of a white peony. Scrape and cut in pieces an inch square. Eat one three times a day, never taking any food after four P.M. Use one month, stop two weeks, and begin again. — *Eighteenth-century herbal.*

Onions reduce hypertension, high blood sugar, cholesterol, and the fat content of the blood.

Use yarrow or lemon balm to staunch blood flow.

A mixture of mashed mistletoe leaves and milk dissolves blood clots.

One ounce of crushed watermelon seeds, steeped in boiling water, reduces high blood pressure.

Pregnancy, Childbirth, and Menstrual Cramps

Chamomile tea relieves all kinds of cramps.

Drink raspberry tea for painful menstruation and aid in childbirth.

Sage tea reduces nursing mothers' milk flow when weaning.

Use tarragon to bring on menstruation.

Drink peony tea for pregnancy. (Superstition holds that if you gather peony for medicinal purposes while a woodpecker is in sight, your patient might die.)

Wallflower increases a woman's fertility and eases pain during childbirth.

The brew from boiling mistletoe is good for fertility.

Childbirth will be easier if a woman drinks raspberry tea and sleeps with an ax under her pillow.

Burns

Take one pound of primrose leaves. Crush in a mortar with half a pound of the flowers. Simmer in hog's lard until crisp. Strain for ulcers or burns.

Strip fresh elder flowers from the stalks, simmer in hog's lard, strain and use on the face and neck when sunburned.

Apply a poultice made from burdock or comfrey.

Use an ointment made from calendula flowers.

Take an infusion made from witch hazel.

Stomachaches and Indigestion

Drink blackberry juice or raspberry tea for diarrhea.

Basil tea, catnip tea, and dandelion tea are good treatments for bowel regularity.

Drink lavender tea for intestinal gas.

Try mint tea and onion juice for gas pains.

Pumpkin seeds expel intestinal worms.

Use rosemary oil for gas.

Rose water can help overindulgence in wine and diseases of the stomach.

Anise seeds aid digestion.

Try basil to reduce weight.

Dill prevents obesity.

Fennel is good for those who have grown too fat.

Fennel Seed Digestive Tea
Use one to one-and-one-half teaspoons fennel seeds and one cup boiling water. Crush the seeds lightly with a spoon, put them into a teapot, and pour water over them. Allow them to steep for five to seven minutes, then strain into a cup. Relieves gas and intestinal cramping.

General Tonics

Ginseng
Gentian apertif to "comfort the heart"
Borage to drive away melancholy, revive the hypochondriac
Tarragon leaves chewed before taking medicine to dull the taste
Sassafras tea, called saloop, as a cure-all
Borage brings courage (Pliny)
Cordial flowers (rose, violet, alkanet, and borage) to cheer the heart
Lemon balm to restore youth
Chamomile and gentian tea
Blackberry root tea for summer disorders
Pokeweed for spring tonic
Chamomile flower tea for the entire system
Dandelion tea when you feel tired
Eating pickles to cure love sickness

Baldness

Rub onion juice on the bald spot.
Sprinkle parsley seeds on the head three nights of every year.
Rub the head with stinging nettle.

Insomnia

"Chop chamomile and crumbs of brown bread, small, and boyl them with white wine vinegar. Stir it well and spread it on a cloth and binde it to the soles of the feet as hot as you can suffer it." — Eighteenth-century herbal

"Take dried rose leaves, keep them in a glasse which will keep them sweet and then take powder of mint, powder of cloves and put the same to the rose leaves. Put together in a bag and take that to bed with you and it will cause you to sleep and it is good to smell unto at other times." — Herbal, *1606*

Hiccups

Eat cervil seeds soaked in vinegar.
Try dill boiled in wine (the seed is more useful than the leaves).

An apple a day keeps the doctor away. A rosary a day keeps the devil away. An onion a day keeps everybody away.

RECREATING GRANDMA'S GARDEN

Every year during my growing-up years, my family traveled from Atlanta to Jeffersontown, Kentucky, over Easter and on summer vacations. Although the car was crowded with Mom, Dad, and five kids, I don't remember much complaining because we were headed to my grandparents' farm, a magical place for us all.

Vacations with my grandparents were riddled with rituals. The first one was to see who could spot Grandpa's big red barn first as we got close to the farm. Being the fourth and next to the youngest, I rarely won this particular contest, but it never bothered me because by that time we were almost to Grandma's.

The next ritual ensued when we actually pulled in the driveway and spilled out of the car like a bunch of ants. Grandpa would be standing there rubbing his cheek saying, "Well, well, well!" like we were the last people in the world he had expected. Grandma would come out of the kitchen door, wiping floury hands on her apron, saying, "I was getting worried about you. I thought you would be here hours ago." It never mattered when we got there. Grandma always expected us hours before.

Before the grownups were through talking, we kids had disappeared to check our favorite spots. I always went straight for the geranium tree. This was an old hollowed-out tree way back behind the house. Nature had carved a perfect little flower pot out of one of the trunks, and one year Grandpa had surprised me by planting a big, bright red geranium there. I immediately called it my "geranium tree." Every year after that until he died, he remembered to plant a geranium there for me.

Although Grandpa grew the best vegetables in all the world, it was Grandma's flower garden that held me spellbound. Through the eyes of a little girl, it was a fairy land. Sweetly scented, brightly colored blossoms spilled and tumbled over each other, each one trying to outdo the other.

Hollyhocks stood guard along the back fence while sweet peas laughingly climbed up and over and around them. Majestic lilies had a place all their own, but everything else thrived good-naturedly in the ghetto of the garden. Like her mother's garden before her, my grandmother's combined herbs, vegetables, and flowers. The result was a riot of color and a cornucopia of scents.

Bright red zinnias were among my favorites, for they withstood the hot Kentucky summers without complaining. They rarely drooped and almost always looked fresh and ready for picking. Perhaps these were my favorites because Grandma allowed me to pick a handful to take upstairs to my room.

Marigolds were planted near the tomatoes, garlic by the rose bushes. Mint was everywhere, its scent pervasive.

Because my grandpa loved dahlias, Grandma grew huge, prize-winning specimens. She also grew deep red cockscomb in honor and memory of my great-grandmother, who always kept these in her parlor.

When I finally had the place and time to create a garden of my own, I wanted it to look just like my grandmother's. Although her garden was country and informal, everyone's grandmother put an indelible mark on each of us and our concept of the garden: some formal colonial revival, some Victorian, some similar to pioneer gardens. The development of the American garden, like much else American, was the result of a melting pot, derived from a combination of influences: some European, some native American, some unique to those people called Americans. Today we plant many different kinds of "old-fashioned gardens," each authentic and uniquely American. The old-fashioned garden you choose depends on your locale, your resources, your personal preference, and, of course, your favorite memories.

EARLY SPANISH

The earliest of all gardens planted in the New World were created by the Spanish in Florida. In 1565 the governor imported tools, seeds, and plants to fashion the many gardens and orchards that graced the settlements by 1600. The best gardeners were probably the priests in the missions, for the majority of other settlers were military men with little time or interest in gardening. The gardens were usually part of a patio setting and were surrounded by a group of buildings or high walls. The Spanish were also instrumental in establishing gardens and homes along the West Coast, particularly in what is now California. These gardens were sometimes surrounded by prickly pear hedges, which grew as tall as twenty feet.

SETTLER GARDENS

While Spanish settlers were struggling to get oranges and lemons established in their gardens in the south, Puritan housewives were planting medicinal herbs, fruits, and vegetables to help sustain their families through another harsh Massachusetts winter. Usually the men tended the fields and orchard, leaving the kitchen garden the sole

The garden at Buena Ventura far exceeded anything I had before met with in this region, both in respect of the quality, quantity, and variety of its excellent productions, not only indigenous to the country, but appertaining to the temperate as well as the torrid zone. — *George Vancouver, English navigator, 1793*

domain of the housewife.

The colonists found useful plants already growing in their new land, many of which proved to be of great value nutritionally and medicinally. It is hard to imagine the importance of English seeds and plants to these first colonists. The slips of flowers, herbs, and vegetables sent from home were crucial to the health and happiness of the new colonies. Each arriving ship was met with great hopes that seeds and roots had arrived in good shape. William Logan, a settler from Germantown, ordered seeds from England in 1749. Along with his order he included the following instructions: "Take care the mise don't Eat them . . . don't lett the Salt water wash them." His fears were well-grounded. Sea voyages were long and dangerous, and little care was taken to preserve correctly these precious bits of plant life.

Gardens in Europe during the late sixteenth and early seventeenth centuries were marked by elaborate design and the need for meticulous and constant care. These gardens were embroidery-like patterns of closely clipped herbs with grey and green leaves or low-growing hedges made into knots and mazes. But to the Puritans trying to carve a bit of cultivated sanity out of the wilderness, practicality was the foremost consideration in a garden. Gardens in the early days of New England were of vital importance to each household for the settlers were ever aware of the link between food in the garden and their own survival.

The size of the garden depended on the size of the family. Although not every garden contained flowers, all had common vegetables such as leeks, onions, garlic, melons, English gourds, radishes, carrots, cabbages, artichokes, and pumpkins.

Gardens were laid out without concern for symmetry or design. Plants were placed where they received the best soil and the greatest amount of sunlight. Generally, gardens were surrounded by paling or picket fences to exclude livestock and wild animals. Fencing was strictly regulated in these early settlements. Among other things, fences were needed as proof of ownership of land. Early Connecticut law required a "five rayle or equal to it," and in Virginia the fencing had to be of paling seven-and-a-half feet high. Although fencing around kitchen garden plots was relatively formal, fencing around planting fields was much less so. One popular type was the "worm," or "zigzag," where logs or poles were laid horizontally on upright posts to form a zigzag pattern.

The Puritan housewife arranged her garden with regard to those things that would come back year after year (perennials) and those which she would have to replant yearly (annuals.) She planted close to the house whatever she would need to put her hands on instantly: common medicinal herbs or herbs for flavoring and seasoning. She kept big rooted things (carrots, potatoes, and onions) separate from those with delicate roots (lettuce and spinach). Some herbs she used

Throughout the seventeenth century [the housewife] must be able to extract from [the garden] all she would need for flavorings and seasonings and garnishes, for insect repellents and deodorants, for changing the air in rooms and keeping out moths and rodents and snakes, for dyeing and fulling and teasing, for concocting and cordials and waters, for making plasters and salves and coated pills, for treating wounds and aiding in childbirths and in laying out the dead. Finally, she must find there her favorite plants, remedies or no, like pansies and pinks and violets with their own familiar country names which only to hear was to be sustained and comforted. —*Ann Leighton,* Early American Gardens, For Meate and Medicine.

For pottage and puddings and custards and pies, Our pumpkins and parsnips are common supplies; We have pumpkin at morning and pumpkin at noon; If it were not for pumpkin we should be undone.

often and planted a great deal of: clove gillyflowers (pinks) for seasoning, elecampane for lung ailments, bugloss as a general antidote, feverfew for fevers, everlasting to keep away moths, tansy for general medicinal purposes, balm for stings, and salad herbs for eating. Flowers, not as immediately essential, were grown further from the house.

Garden walks in New England were scraped and spread with fine gravel, which was then rolled. Though chalk was good for drainage, it was said to be "uneasie for such as wear high-heeled shoes." Sometimes crushed clam shells were used. The walks were usually just wide enough to allow a person to walk easily through the

garden. The central walkway in a formal garden was usually slightly wider.

As the settlers' hold on the land became more secure, flower gardens became a more common sight. The small dooryard, or "parlor," garden became a mark of pride for the housewife. This forerunner of the front yard was usually close to the house, enclosed by a painted fence, and planted with roses, perennials, herbs, and perhaps some scented annuals. Its size and beauty depended on the time and interest a housewife was able to invest in her "parlor" patch.

WILLIAMSBURG AND
THE SOUTHERN PLANTATION GARDENS

Enormous profits from tobacco created a southern lifestyle that persisted until the Civil War. Because time and money were abundant for plantation owners, they became planters of pleasure gardens, many keeping close ties with England, where interest in horticulture was at a fever pitch. Virginians took pride in sending wonderful exotic plants from their evolving gardens back to England. Many southern gardeners imported plants from all over the world. French and African marigolds, globe amaranth, China asters, nasturtiums, and Oriental poppies were favorite import flowers sent to America via England. The ornamental plants of greatest impact on southern gardens were introduced by André Michaux toward the end of the eighteenth century. Michaux traveled the world collecting plants and brought camellias, evergreen azaleas, and crepe myrtle to the South.

The design of large plantation gardens was greatly influenced by popular English landscape architects such as Capability Brown and later Batty Langley. Langley, in particular, with his ideas of naturally curving paths and large open spaces, was of particular importance to George Washington when he was designing Mount Vernon and to Thomas Jefferson in his design of Monticello.

Williamsburg became the royal capital of Virginia in 1699. Gardens in the city were strongly influenced by William and Mary, the ruling English monarchs, who themselves had a keen interest in gardening. Tight, formal gardens were very popular; even when England began to change her gardening habits, colonists in Williamsburg clung to the formal, symmetrical patterns prevalent in England during the time that Williamsburg was established.

Outstanding features of these gardens included "knottes," small hedges of close-growing plants of thrift, thyme, or dwarf boxwood. "Parterres," rectilinear and geometric elaborations of knottes interspersed with stretches of closely cut grass, were also popular as were "compartments," round or oval beds of flowers set among the grass. Most of the gardens at Williamsburg were laid out like miniature plantations, with outbuildings on the outer edges of a formal garden. The colonists welcomed architectural features such as arbors, topiary, espaliered fruit trees, and dovecotes.

A popular garden plan included a long central walk, intersected by crosswalks that divided the garden into a series of squares or rectangles. The walks were generally made of brick or marl, washed pebbles, gravel, broken pieces of stone, or oyster or scallop shells. The gardens were almost always fenced or enclosed by hedges. Post and rail fences were commonly used to surround private gardens while brick walls were used for public buildings. "Quick-set" hedges, also popular, were made by digging a ditch and planting quick-growing shrubs, such as hawthorn and privet.

TURN-OF-THE-CENTURY GARDENS

Until well into the nineteenth century, the average American had little time or effort to put into gardening. The plantation gardens of the South and the estate gardens of the North were planted and enjoyed by the wealthy while "just folks" had to settle for a few plants set outside the kitchen door.

The rapid rise of wealth and population in America during the late nineteenth and early twentieth centuries gave rise to a middle class with both time and money. The birth of the middle class led, in turn, to great interest in gardening and town and community beautification. Garden design of middle-class Americans during this period was similar to that of the first settler gardens. Flowers, vegetables, herbs, and fruit were planted where they grew best and were most convenient. As early as 1840 the health benefits of gardening were recommended to women, who were being urged to adapt a more "physical lifestyle." Gardening was thought to be a necessary component of this new lifestyle because it was "stimulating and not strenuous," according to a popular nineteenth-century magazine: "This taste, which leads them into open air, under bright and healthful skies—this labor, not severe, but gently exciting, which gives to exercise a meaning and a pleasure, which no forced walks or obligatory calisthenics ever have or can have."

The years before the Depression were a golden era for landscape architecture in America. Gardens of the wealthy were opulently decked with stonework, statuary, fountains, and pools modeled after European garden artwork. The English influence was equally strong and resulted in rose and perennial plantings after the "cottage garden" style.

GRANDMA'S GARDEN

For the average American gardener, the beauty of the garden still lies in growing simple flowers. The front yard, or dooryard, garden was of prime importance to lovers of flowers and home, for the front yard became a virtual extension of the home. The front yard was almost always enclosed by a fence, the sides of which usually came out from the corners of the house to meet the front portion along the edge of the street. Protected from the trampling feet of children, pets, and livestock, the front yard became a show place for Grandma's most prized flowers.

Spring began with the arrival of the purple crocus, followed quickly by the sweet fragrance of poet's narcissus. Grape hyacinths were found at the base of shrubs, and single yellow and red tulips sometimes put on a gaudy show for a few weeks. Lilacs could be found in every front yard where the climate permitted their cultivation. Syringa, flowering currant, snowberry bushes, spirea, and deutzias all put forth glorious bloom.

Peonies always had a favored place. As the years went by, the peony plants put forth more and more blossoms until finally all else paled in comparison. Phlox, canterbury bells, and day lilies came later in summer. Roses grew all around. A shade tree invariably stood guard just outside the latched gate. The path to the door was edged on both sides with pinks, double white or pink. If the family was well-to-do, twin boxwoods often stood on either side of the door.

To the side of the house and in the back kitchen garden, the rules were more relaxed, the flowers allowed to sprawl and crawl like happy-go-lucky children. It was here that portulaca and petunias clashed in color and scarlet runner bean skinnied up the columns to the porch. Nasturtiums, marigolds, and hollyhocks shouted out in bright and raucous colors.

SUGGESTED PLANTS FOR A GRANDMA'S GARDEN
Spring

hyacinth

peony

tulip

sweet William

daffodil

English daisy

violet (especially white)

crocus

primrose

iris

pansy

forget-me-not

periwinkle

thrift

lily of the valley

columbine

Summer

rose (damask, Provence, moss)

Canterbury bell (pale pink,
    lavender, deep purple, white)

Shirley poppy

cornflower

foxglove (deep purple, pink)

lily (Madonna, tiger)

larkspur (blue)

lemon lily (daylily)

daylily (orange)

iris

hollyhock

chamomile

phlox (white with red or purple
    eye)

four o'clock

canna lily

zinnia

China aster

geranium

PLANTING A PERIOD GARDEN

Planting a garden to represent a historical period can be a rewarding and exciting hobby. The everyday rituals of nurturing plants and seedlings are made meaningful by tradition and historical association. Many different factors have to be considered when planting a period garden, and planning should begin well in advance of actual planting.

The following questions need to be answered:

(1) How authentic to the period do you want to be? Gardens from the past did not have the benefit of chemical fertilizers and pesticides. Although this did make for a healthier environment, it also sometimes resulted in a garden that looked quite different from today's, not only in the kinds of plants used but also how the plants looked. To be truly authentic it will be important to use only plants, fencing materials, fertilizers, pesticides, and equipment available to those gardeners who actually lived during the period you hope to recreate. For example, before 1860 rotary or reel mowers were not available, and lawns were cut with a hand scythe. Prior to 1900 gravel was the most common material for garden walks in the North; brick, in the South.

(2) If you are restoring a garden in conjunction with a house, what kind of garden was actually used originally? Although a colonial house suggests a formal colonial garden, did the former occupants actually have this type of garden? Were they a family of means who could afford the planting and upkeep of such grounds? Could they afford to import flowers and bulbs from Europe, or did they need to rely on native American plants? Look at the house itself. Is it elegant or simple? What kind of lifestyle did these people have? Were they austere and strict, indicating a garden more for sustenance than pleasure? Were they garden lovers? Did they take time and trouble with their garden?

There are many ways to find the answers to these questions. Some information will be available in old records at the library or county courthouse. Look at scrapbooks from families, garden clubs, and civic organizations in the community. Read diaries and personal letters and look for any paintings of the house and grounds. In late fall when the tall grass has died down, poke around to see what you can discover. You might find pieces of an old wall or depressions indicating planting beds. If you are truly interested, don't leave a stone unturned.

(3) Is this really what the garden looked like? There are many common pitfalls in establishing period gardens. Say "old-fashioned" to some people and they take it as a free ticket to junk up their gardens. Plants that are old are not necessarily appropriate. Quaint well houses, ox yokes, barrels, jugs, and old farm tools have their place, but not in your well-tended nineteenth-century garden. Foundation plantings are a twentieth-century introduction and should not be used in an

authentic garden reproduction or restoration.

In spite of their great appeal today, separate herb gardens did not exist in earlier centuries, unless they were planted for a specific reason, such as the medicinal garden at Old Salem in North Carolina. Herbs, vegetables, and flowers were almost always planted together. *(4) How much of the garden or estate can you realistically plant?* Rudy Favretti suggests in *For Every House a Garden* that if you own only a portion of an original estate, you should not try to condense all of the landscape features and fit them onto your parcel. To stay authentic, it is important to keep to the same scale as the original estate, even if it means not planting everything you want to include.

delphinium
petunia
snapdragon
gladiolus
yucca

Trees

redbud (Judas tree)
flowering almond
flowering peach
wild cherry
oaks
sycamore
Eastern red cedar

Shrubs

snowball bush
chinaberry
oak-leaf hydrangea
hibiscus
quince
kerria rose

Vines

jasmine (Carolina white)
morning glory
cross-vine
honeysuckle
wisteria

A Gateway of the "Friendly Little Garden" Where "all the short paths are of irregular stepping-stones; these require much time for clipping but their beauty warrants it, for wild Violets and English Daisies spring up all about them." *At a home in Maywood, Illinois*

HELP FOR TODAY'S OLD-FASHIONED GARDENER

Interest in old-fashioned gardens and garden history is increasing. Throughout the country gardeners are beginning to realize not only the importance of saving and growing heirloom plants, but also the fun and joy of growing the same kinds of plants that Grandma did.

With the resurgence of interest comes help for the enthusiast. The following resources should be of help to those interested in establishing a period garden or restoring an old garden.

SOCIETIES AND ORGANIZATIONS

**The Thomas Jefferson Center
    for Historic Plants**
Mr. John T. Fitzpatrick,
    Director
Monticello
P.O. Box 316
Charlottesville, VA 22902

**Alliance for Historic
    Landscape Preservation**
82 Wall Street, Suite 1105
New York, NY 10005

**The Southern Garden History
    Society**
Old Salem, Inc.
Drawer F
Salem Station
Winston Salem, NC 27108

The Heritage Roses Group
RD 1 Box 299
Clinton Corners, NY 12514

**The Historic Preservation
    Committee, ASLA**
Landscapes
Box 2425 Saugatuck Station
Westport, CT 06880

The Trellis
Horticultural Heritage
    Committee
San Diego Historical Society
1330 31st Street
San Diego, CA 92102

**Bulletin of American
    Garden History**
P.O. Box 397A Planetarium
    Station
New York, NY 10024
(last published in 1987)

**Living Historical Farms
    Bulletin**
Living Historical Farms and
    Agricultural Museums
Smithsonian Institution
Washington, DC 20560

**Friends of Historic
    Landscapes Directory**
Alicia Weber
Park Historic Architectures
    Division
National Park Service
P.O. Box 37127
Washington, DC 20013-7127

LIVING HISTORY MUSEUMS

For a complete list of Living History Farms and Museums, write the Smithsonian Institution, Washington, DC 20560

The Cooper Historic Garden
472 Gibson Avenue
Pacific Grove, CA 93950

Georgia Agrirama
Box Q
Tifton, GA 31794

Grove Farm Homestead
Box 1631
Lihue, HI 96766

Living History Farms
2600 NW 111th Street
Des Moines, IA 50322

The Homeplace
Land Between the Lakes
Tennessee Valley Authority
Golden Pond, KY 42231

Norlands
Washburn-Norlands
Foundation
Box 3395 RD 2
Livermore Falls, ME 04254

National Colonial Farm
3400 Bryan Point Road
Accokeek, MD 20607

**Freeman Farm at Old
    Sturbridge Village**
Sturbridge, MA 01566

Plimouth Plantation
Box 1620
Plymouth, MA 02360

Fortenberry Parkman Farm
1150 Lankeland Drive
Jackson, MS 39216

Old Cienega Village
Route 2 Box 214
Santa Fe, NM 87501

Philipsburg Manor
150 White Plains Road
Tarrytown, NY 10591

Hale Farm and Village
2686 Oak Hill Road
Bath, OH 44210

Quiet Valley
Box 2495 RD 2
Stroudsburg, PA 18360

Old World Wisconsin
Route 2 Box 18
Eagle, WI 53119

SEED COMPANIES AND SEED AND PLANT EXCHANGES

The Olde Thyme Flower and Seed Herbal Exchange
Barbara Pond
415 1st Corso
Nebraska City, NE 68410

A Heritage Seed Program
Canadian Organic Growers
Heather Apple
RR 3
Uxbridge, ON
Canada L0C 1K0

Alston Seed Growers
Littleton, NC 27851
Catalog $1.00
(Rare old-time non-hybrid corn)

Antique Rose Emporium
Route 5, Box 143
Brenham, TX 77833
Catalog $2.00
(Old garden roses)

Applesource
Route 1
Chapin, IL 62628
Catalog free
(Service that sends unusual varieties of antique apples to taste before you plant)

Arbor and Espalier
201 Buena Vista Avenue East
San Francisco, CA 94117
Catalog free
(Old-fashioned and unusual apples and pears)

Bountiful Gardens
19550 Walker Road
Willits, CA 95490
Catalog free
(Open pollinated vegetable seeds)

Burford Brothers
Monroe, VA 24574
Write for information
(Antique and modern apples)

Color Farm Growers
2710 Thornhill Road
Auburndale, FL 33823
Catalog 50¢
(Old-fashioned heirloom types of coleus)

Corns
Route 1 Box 32
Turpin, OK 73950
Catalog $1.00
(Open-pollinated corn)

Country Bloomer's Nursery
20091 East Chapman Avenue
Orange, CA 92669
Catalog free
(Old garden and miniature roses)

The Flower and Herb Exchange
604 North Street
Decorah, IA 52101
Catalog $3.00
(Seed exchange for old-fashioned flowers and herbs)

Forevergreen Farm
70 New Gloucester Road
North Yarmouth, ME 04021
Catalog free
(Old-fashioned, hardy roses)

Fox Hill Farm
525 Fowler Road
Newcastle, CA 95658
Write for information
(Herbs, scented geraniums, bee and dye plants)

Fox Hollow Herbs
P.O. Box 148
McGrann, PA 16236
(Open-pollinated herbs and vegetables)

The Fragrant Path
P.O. Box 328
Ft. Calhoun, NE 68023
Catalog $1.00
(Fragrant, rare, and old-fashioned plants)

Garden City Seeds
P.O. Box 297
Victor, MT 59875
(Heirloom and open-pollinated seeds, vegetables, flowers)

Good Hollow Greenhouse
Route 1, Box 116
Taft, TN 38488
Catalog $1.00
(Herbs, perennials, scented geraniums, and wildflowers)

Good Seed Company
Star Route, Box 73 A
Oroville, WA 98844
Catalog $1.00
(Heirloom vegetable seeds)

Goodwin Creek Gardens
P.O. Box 83
Williams, OR 97544
Catalog $1.00
(Everlasting annual and perennial flowers, herbs, wildflowers)

Greenmantle Nursery
3010 Ettersburg Road
Garberville, CA 95440
Catalog $2.00
(Antique apples, old garden roses)

Hartman's Herb Farm
Old Dana Road
Barre, MA 01005
Catalog $1.00
(Herb and scented geranium plants)

Heirloom Garden Seed
P.O. Box 138
Guerneville, CA 95446
Catalog $2.00
(Culinary herbs and heirloom flowers)

Heirloom Seeds
P.O. Box 245
West Elizabeth, PA 15088-0245
(Heirloom vegetables)

Heritage Gardens
1 Meadow Ridge Road
Shenandoah, IA 51602
Catalog free
(Perennials, flowering trees, and shrubs)

Heritage Rosarium
211 Haviland Mill Road
Brookvill, MD 20833
Catalog $1.00
(Old garden and modern shrub and species roses)

Heritage Rose Gardens
16831 Mitchell Creek Drive
Ft. Bragg, CA 95437
Catalog $1.00
(Heritage and old garden roses)

High Altitude Gardens
P.O. Box 4619
620 Sun Valley Road
Ketchum, ID 83340
Catalog $2.00
(Gourmet and heirloom vegetables, herbs)

High Country Rosarium
1717 Downing Street
Denver, CO 80209
Catalog $1.00
(Old garden roses)

Historical Roses
1657 West Jackson Street
Painesville, OH 44077
Catalog long SASE
(Old garden roses)

Johnson Nursery
Route 5
Ellijay, GA 30540
Catalog free
(Old apple and peach varieties)

D. Landreth Seed Company
P.O. Box 6426
180 West Ostend Street
Baltimore, MD 21230
Catalog $2.00
(New and old varieties of vegetables, herbs, garden annuals)

Lawson's Nursery
Route 1 Box 472
Yellow Creek Road
Ball Ground, GA 30107
Catalog free
(Antique apple and pear trees)

Le Champion Heritage Seeds
P.O. Box 1602
Freedom, CA 95019-1602
Catalog $1.00

Lowe's Own-root Roses
6 Sheffield Road
Nashua, NH 03062
(Old roses)

National Heirloom Flower Seed Exchange
136 Irving Street
Cambridge, MA 02138
Catalog long SASE

Ozark National Seed Order
P.O. Box 932
Woodstock, NY 12498
Catalog 50¢
(Untreated garden seeds)

Redwood City Seed Company
P.O. Box 361
Redwood City, CA 94064
Catalog $1.00
(Open pollinated vegetables and herbs, most developed before 1906)

Rose Acres
6641 Crystal Boulevard
Diamond Springs, CA 95619
Catalog long SASE
(Old roses)

Roses of Yesterday and Today
802 Brown's Valley Road
Watsonville, CA 95076-0398
Catalog $3.00
(Old garden roses)

Sanctuary Seeds/Folklore Herb Company, Ltd.
2388 W. 4th Avenue
Vancouver, BC
Canada V6K 1P1
Catalog $1.00
(Open-pollinated and untreated vegetable and herb seeds)

Seeds Blum
Idaho City Stage
Boise, ID 83706
Catalog $2.00
(Vegetables, annuals, perennials)

Seed Source/Sharp Plants
Route 2, Box 265C
Asheville, NC 28805
Catalog $3.00

Select Seeds
81 Stickney Hill Road
Union, CT 06076
Catalog $2.00
(Old-fashioned and heirloom perennials)

Southern Exposure Seed Exchange
P.O. Box 158
North Garden, VA 22959
Catalog $3.00
(Heirloom vegetables)

Southern Seeds
P.O. Box 2091
Melbourne, FL 32902
Catalog $1.00
(Open-pollinated vegetables for hot climates)

Talavaya Seeds
Route 2, Box 2
36A Tesiqie Drive
Espanola, NM 87532
Catalog $1.00
(Open-pollinated corn, beans, melons, squash, amaranth, peppers, and quinoa)

Thompson and Morgan
P.O. Box 1308
Jackson, NJ 08527
Catalog free
(Annuals, perennials, vegetables)

Yesterday's Rose
572 Las Colindas Road
San Rafael, CA 94903
Catalog $2.00
(Old garden and modern shrub roses)

CHILDREN IN THE GARDEN

I think that my grandmother was happiest when she was sharing her garden with a child. She had a whole slew of grandchildren who benefited from her love of flowers. But we all lived in different towns and were not always available when Grandma wanted to share garden treasures with a little person.

Finding a child was never a problem for Grandma, for they were attracted to her like bees to a flower. Sunday school children and neighbors' kids found their way through the garden gate and into Grandma's fairyland of flowers. She had endless patience with these children, explaining how to plant a seed, how to nurture the plants as they grew, and finally how to harvest the products of their labor.

Grandma believed that the garden was the perfect place to enjoy a child. Here it is easy to see the glory of God and witness the wonders of nature. Grandma believed that the fertile soil of the garden cultivated not only flowers and vegetables, but also emotions and impressions that cause children to develop a lifelong love of and sensitivity to the world of nature.

Emma Denton of Hiawassee, Georgia, says her mother got her interested in flowers when she was just six or seven. "Mama used to wear one of those long old aprons, and she used to tell me to go out and dig up a bed about the size of her apron. So I did, and she used to tell everybody that every one of those flower beds would fit her apron just exactly.

"I grew nasturtiums, marigolds, touch-me-nots, zinnias, and a lot more in those apron-sized beds. And I just loved doing it. I used to go down to the barn where the chickens roosted and get some of that old, rich dirt for my flower beds."

For a child with a spot of soil and a willing and understanding adult to share it with, a garden can truly be a miraculous experience. Rosalind Creasy writes in *Earthly Delights* that she treated her childhood garden just like her dollhouse, constantly rearranging everything. "I seldom produced anything, and most of my plants died because they were weary from being moved. Nevertheless, I have wonderful memories of 'gardening' with my father. Looking back on that experience, I can see what an ideal environment it was for learning."

When helping a child with his or her garden, quick and guaranteed results play an important role. Seeds like sunflowers are particularly satisfactory because the plants get big so quickly. Sunflowers have the added benefit of providing food for birds and little children when they go to seed.

Pumpkins can also grow to be huge, much to the delight of the child who planted the seed. When the pumpkin fruit is about half grown, help the child scratch out his name on its surface. Use a ballpoint pen and scratch no more than one-eighth inch deep. Space the letters about one inch apart to give them room to grow as the pumpkin grows. By harvest time the child's name will be clear on the surface of the fruit.

Pole beans are wonderful for growing into a "bean tepee." Place poles or sticks in the shape of a tepee and plant bean seeds at the base of each pole. As the plants emerge and begin to grow, train the vines up the poles. By the end of the summer the child will have a living tepee. Other vegetables that are easy and rewarding include potatoes, strawberries, mint, radishes, and squash.

Several different garden crafts are fun for children. For example, use flower petals as crayons. Take brightly colored petals and rub them on a piece of white paper. The pigment in the petals will rub off onto the paper. Use leaves to draw green grass, cornflowers for blue sky, and pink petunias for fluffy clouds.

My own son, David, was born shortly before my grandmother became too ill to garden. When he was a few months old, I took him to visit her. When we arrived, Grandma scooped David up, and I saw very little of him for the remainder of our visit. Almost as if she sensed that her time with this new great-grandson would be short, she was with him constantly, feeding and bathing him and rocking him to sleep.

But when David wasn't crying for food or sleep, Grandma walked him in the garden. Up and down the paths they would go, David resting peacefully in Grandma's arms. Only his tiny infant ears heard the words of wisdom that Grandma spoke to him, only he could hear the love in her voice as she introduced him to her favorite flowers and told him stories of where they came from and how they had made their way into her garden.

When she died a few years later, I remembered that special visit David had with her and often wonder what spell she wove that week. For David has grown up to have a true kinship with nature and his connection to the physical world is an essential part of who he is. Part of it, I know, is a child's natural curiosity and love of nature. But I can't help but wonder if another part of it came from his great-grandmother.

The beautifully balanced cycles of nature have always brought a sense of peace and tranquility to me, and my grief at my grandmother's death was eased by my love for my son and daughter. It is only right that as one generation passes, the next comes. It is a story that Grandma taught me in her garden long ago. The seeds grow and produce fruit. The fruits turn to seeds that fall and grow once again. It is a never-ending cycle, a never-ending story.